The Whitworth Society

SIR JOSEPH WHITWORTH, BART.

1803 - 1887

Presented to

Thomas John Bennett

on the occasion of the 36th Whitworth Awards Presentation Ceremony at the Institution of Mechanical Engineers by the President of the Whitworth Society

James Potten WSch

26 September 2019

Miscellaneous Papers On Mechanical Subjects

MISCELLANEOUS PAPERS

ON

MECHANICAL SUBJECTS.

GUNS AND STEEL,

BY SIR JOSEPH WHITWORTH, BART.,

C.E., F.R.S., LL.D., D.C.L.

LONDON:

LONGMANS, GREEN, READER, & DYER.

1873.

1876, Oct. 17.
Farrar Fund.

PRINTED BY GEORGE FALKNER AND SON, IMPERIAL BUILDINGS, DEANSGATE, MANCHESTER.

PREFACE.

1.—The following pages give an account of my system of rifled guns, and show how it originated and has been developed.

2.—In the application of this system to guns of large calibre I was led to the manufacture of steel, and found that by subjecting the metal to extreme pressure when in a fluid state I could produce steel of absolute soundness.

3.—Having always contended that guns should be made of steel, I have now removed every *practical* objection to the use of that material, and I reject as utterly unsuitable in their manufacture the combination of a weak and a strong metal, such as iron and steel. It will be seen on referring to the experiments detailed in this work that it is possible to make guns of ductile steel possessing twice the strength of iron, and completely master of the gunpowder. My breech-loading gun, made of *fluid-compressed* steel, with its large powder chamber, cannot burst or break up into pieces. For penetration and destructive power it will fire shells of such length and capacity as no one would venture to use for a gun of mixed iron and steel, while its range will be at high elevations from 45 to 50 per cent. greater than that of a muzzle-loading service gun of the same calibre.

4.—It is probable that few are aware of the manner in which I approached the subject of rifling guns, or know that the Whitworth rifle was produced as the result of many months of experimental research in the rifle gallery, five hundred yards long, erected in my grounds at Manchester. I cannot mention this fact without saying how much personal interest the then Commander-in-Chief, Lord Hardinge, took in the experiments, every stage of which he communicated to the Prince Consort. At that time I demonstrated every conclusion by the most carefully conducted trials, and I proved that the Enfield service rifle of that day was wrong in every particular. The diameter of the bullet was too large for the size of the gun, the bullet itself was too short, and the twist of rifling was not one-third of what it should have been. Accordingly, in the year 1857, the public trials of my rifle against the Enfield rifle, made by the direction of Lord Panmure, established the superiority of my weapon, as well as the soundness of the conclusions at which I had arrived.

5.—In 1859 a Committee of officers reported that the bore of my muzzle-loading rifle was too small for use as a military weapon.

6.—In 1869 another Committee recommended that the bore of the service breech-loading rifle should be exactly that rejected ten years previously.

7.—In 1857 I proved for the first time that a ship could be penetrated below the water line by a *flat-headed* rifled projectile.

8.—In 1860 I penetrated for the first time a 4½-inch armour plate with an 80-lbs. *flat-headed solid* steel projectile.

9.—In 1862 I penetrated for the first time a 4-inch armour plate with a 70-lbs. *flat-headed steel shell,* which exploded in an oak box supporting the plate.

10.—In 1870 I penetrated, with a 9-inch bore gun three 5-inch armour plates interlaminated with two 5-inch layers of iron concrete.

11.—In 1872, with my new 9-pounder breech-loading gun and a flat-headed steel projectile, I penetrated a 3-inch armour plate at an angle of 45°.

12.—All these performances were the first of their kind and were made, with one exception, with *flat-headed* projectiles, which alone are capable of penetrating an armour-plate when impinging obliquely; only such projectiles can penetrate a ship below the water line. Yet it will appear that every service projectile has a pointed head, which renders it comparatively useless except for direct fire, and prevents the possibility of penetration below the water line. Hitherto, all Ordnance Committees have abstained from carrying out experiments with flat-headed projectiles. The importance of this subject is, however, so great that it cannot be postponed much longer.

13.—The history of my labours for the last 15 years is now made known in a connected form. I am content to state what I have done and to give the reasons which have influenced me in practice. Hereafter, I hope that progress of mechanical science among those who advise the Minister may enable them to better appreciate the value of a system which is mechanically right, and that the improvements that I have established in the construction of rifled guns, and in producing a material which is capable of developing their powers, may no longer be disregarded.*

14.—A long illness from which I have suffered has delayed the preparation of this work.

* I have also in hand an Appendix to these pages, which will contain extracts of my correspondence with eminent authorities and with the Government.

CHAPTER I.

I PURPOSE in the present work to give some account of my fluid-compressed steel, and to explain the mechanical principles which, in my opinion, should govern the construction of rifled guns.

I have always considered that steel when made of the best materials, and obtained sound, with the relative degree of ductility and strength required, is the best material for guns.

The primary condition being that the steel used for guns should be absolutely sound, the next is that it should possess sufficient ductility. In order to obtain it of the requisite ductility, and of a structure which can be depended on for being absolutely sound, extreme pressure must be applied to the metal when in a fluid state. There is no other process known by which sound ductile steel can be produced in large masses.

DEFECTS OF CAST STEEL.

When highly carburized steel (such as tool steel) is cast in small ingots, and the air and gases escape readily by what is termed "piping," about three-fourths of the length of the ingot will be sound and free from air cells.

If an attempt be made to cast a very large ingot of highly carburized steel, the lower portion may appear sound, as in the smaller ingot, but a new defect and difficulty arises from the fact that the material may crack and destroy itself in the act of cooling.

The outside of the ingot sets first, and the inside portion is therefore exposed to a great strain while cooling; this strain may cause some part to crack or become unsound by reason of the hard unyielding character of the metal.

When guns of the ordinary weight are made of highly carburized steel, there can be no question but that the material is so strong that it will, if sound, completely master the gunpowder. There remains, however, this danger of cracking and unsoundness in cooling which can never be entirely got rid of, and it must also be borne in mind that the material is hard and unyielding, and gives no notice before bursting. It is impossible therefore to manufacture a large gun of highly carburized steel, which can be relied upon as being absolutely sound.

The result of the breaking up of a gun made of hard steel would be terrific; such accidents have happened, and hard steel guns are unsafe.

The safeguard consists in employing steel possessing a higher ductility than tool steel; the material is not so strong, but the danger of breaking up is entirely overcome when the steel is free from air cells.

The more ductile the metal the larger and more numerous are the air cells, and the value of fluid compression becomes proportionately greater.

It may be shown by experiment that steel, which is so ductile that it will elongate from 30 to 35 per cent. before breaking, will bulge and tear under the action of pressure, and will not fly into pieces. In order to ensure this ductility the amount of carbon present in the steel must be comparatively small.

When ductile steel, that is steel so far carburized as to have a ductility represented by 35 per cent. of elongation, is cast into an ingot, it is found in practice that nearly the whole length of the ingot will be subject to honeycomb or air cells and will be unsound.

This is shown by the drawings of an ingot 9 feet in length, weighing 7.3 tons. In order to exhibit the structure of the whole length of the ingot, it was grooved longitudinally to the depth of the plane edges, and was split open by wedges forced in by hydraulic pressure.

The whole of the central portion, with the exception of about 18 inches at the bottom, is unsound from the presence of air cells.

INGOT CAST WITHOUT PRESSURE.

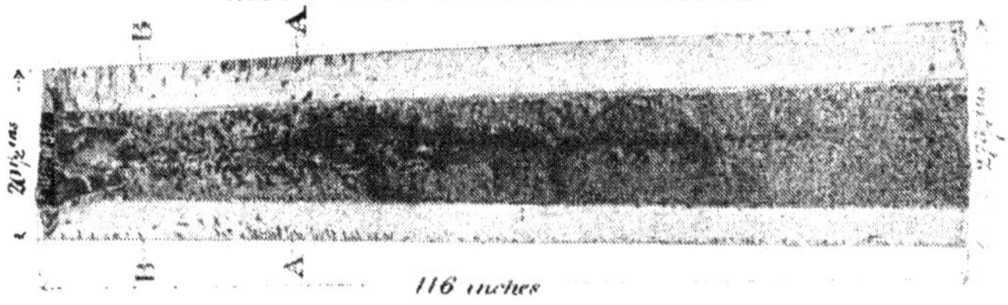

TONS CWTS.
WEIGHT OF INGOT 7 6

ENLARGED THROUGH A A

SECTION THROUGH B B

The conclusion is, that if the steel be soft, the presence of air cells renders a large casting unsound; if the steel be hard, there is danger of cracking, and in neither case can a gun made of steel of the ordinary manufacture be relied on.

The method of testing the ductility of steel will be readily understood from the annexed drawings.

A cylinder of steel is prepared, 2 inches in length in the central part D, and .7979 of an inch in diameter, the cross sectional area being .5 of a square inch. Such a cylinder is shown at A, the ends of the specimen being

D

A 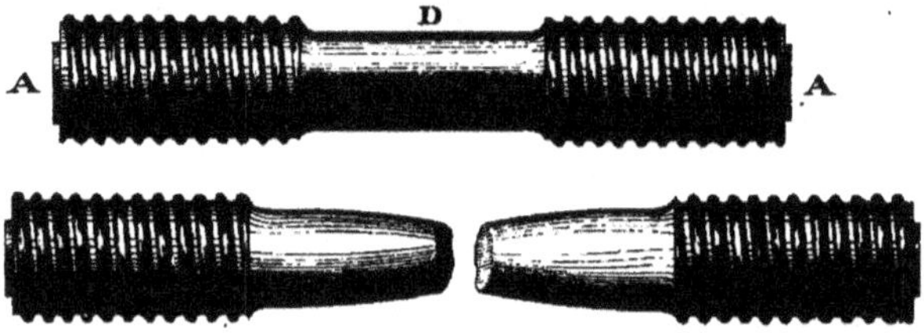 A

B C

screwed in order that the hydraulic apparatus used for pulling it asunder may be readily applied. The portions of A are shown at B and C after the specimen has been pulled into two pieces by the hydraulic pressure. The difference in length before and after the pulling asunder represents the elongation or ductility of the material.

By this method I have found the tensile strength of Bowling and Lowmoor wrought iron to be 27 tons, with a ductility of 38 per cent.; the tensile strength of the Northamptonshire iron being 27 tons, with 28 per cent. of ductility; that of Staffordshire iron being 24 tons, with 30 per cent. of ductility. The tensile strength of good cast iron is 10 tons, with a ductility of 0.75 per cent.

The tensile strength and ductility of fluid-compressed steel are given on page 18.

Hollow Cylinders of Fluid-Compressed Steel.

I have stated that the difficulty of obtaining a large and sound casting of ductile steel may be successfully overcome by applying extreme pressure to the fluid metal.

The castings used for guns are made in the form of hollow cylinders, and the steel is subjected when in a fluid state to great pressure, amounting in some cases to 20 tons on the square inch; the air and gases are driven out from the inside as well as the outside of the cylinder, the hollow form favours both the cooling and the escape of the gases, and the metal is compressed into a perfectly solid and homogeneous body, absolutely sound throughout its entire length, free from air cells, and uniform both in strength and ductility.

The differences between the structure of an ingot of ductile steel, when cast in the usual manner, and when subjected to pressure while in a fluid state, are shown by the drawing, which represents the transverse sections of two ingots about 10 inches square.

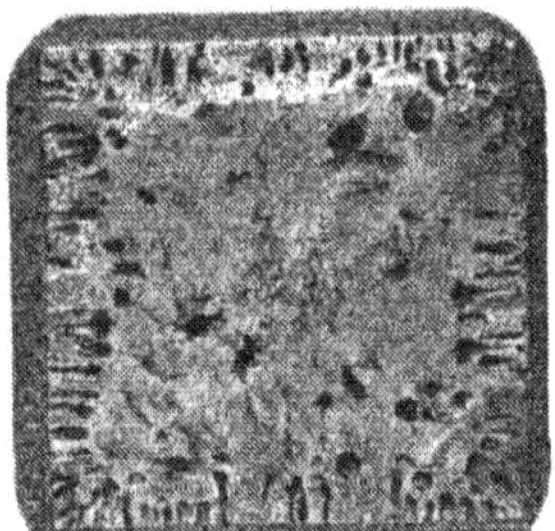

TRANSVERSE SECTION OF STEEL INGOT CAST IN THE ORDINARY WAY.

TRANSVERSE SECTION OF STEEL INGOT COMPRESSED WHILE IN A FLUID STATE.

Within five minutes after the pressure is applied, the fluid column will be shortened by $1\frac{1}{8}$ inches per foot of length. This fact will give some idea of the quantity of air which has been expelled, and which, if present in the metal, would have caused unsoundness.

When ductile steel is cast under the pressure which just suffices to make it sound and free from air cells, it is deficient in strength, and requires to be drawn out and forged in order to develop in a higher degree the strength of the material.

With a pressure of 20 tons on the inch, the fluid-compressed steel becomes as strong and as ductile as if it had been forged.

In the manufacture of compressed steel guns, I draw out and forge the hollow cylinders after they have been cast under pressure.

There is a great future for a material which ensures absolute soundness, especially as applied to large constructions. When the axles for railway carriages and the tyres of wheels are properly made of ductile steel, there can be no accidents from their breakage. Capt. Tyler states in his report that 14 per cent. of the accidents upon railways are caused by broken axles or broken tyres. All such accidents are absolutely preventible by the use of fluid-compressed steel.

In the case of marine engines, sound ductile steel should be used for all the working parts. Thus, a solid propeller shaft, which weighs 12 tons when made of wrought iron, might be replaced by a hollow steel shaft weighing 6 tons.

This fact is probably understated, for at the present time the margin of extra weight to cover possible unsoundness is so great, that we have no data for determining how far we may go in lightening a propeller shaft.

Again, I propose to reduce the weight of a railway carriage from 7 tons to 5 tons, by using steel instead of wrought iron, and in some instances by substituting steel for wood. I have ascertained that during the life of a railway carriage, every ton of dead weight which is saved, produces a saving of £300. Greater security in travelling and increased dividends will satisfy both the public and shareholders.

Locomotive or other cylindrical boilers will be made of complete cylinders instead of riveted plates, and the pressure of the steam may then be doubled or trebled with perfect safety. The economy which would result from the use of sound ductile steel for steam boilers is of the highest importance.

It was at one time most necessary for me to establish by experiment the strength of fluid compressed steel, and, in some of the earlier trials, I relied upon the gunpowder test, which I proceed to describe:—

Cylinders of the metal to be tested, each 4 inches in length, are carefully turned and bored to 1¼ inches external diameter, and ¾-inch internal diameter.

Before testing, the external diameter of the tube is measured in the centre of its length by the Whitworth measuring machine. The tube is then charged with a small quantity of powder in the central space, each end of the tube being filled with beeswax as far as the powder space will permit.

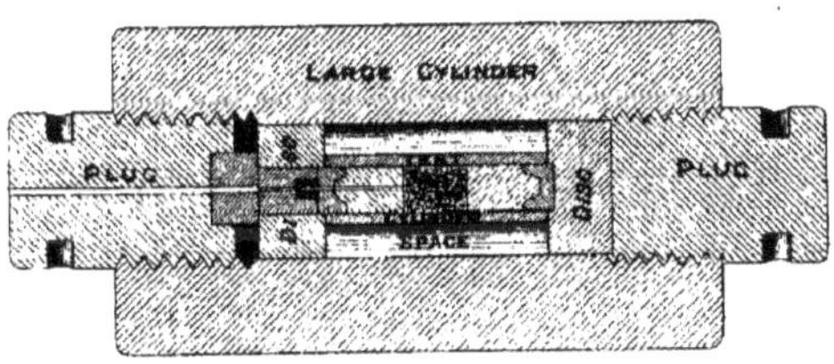

A copper cup, which acts like the cup-leather of a press, closes each end of the cylinder, and the pressure of the powder is received by two flat steel discs held in position by screwed plugs inserted into a massive cylinder, as shown in the drawing.

A small hole or vent passes from the outside into the powder chamber, and allows the ignition of the charge, as well as the escape of the gas. The steel disc through which the vent passes has a conical plug of platinum fitted in its centre, the angle of the cone having been previously determined by experiment, and so adjusted that the wear occasioned by the rush of powder gas will be compensated, and the opening for its escape will not vary.

The powder charges are gradually increased as the tube yields to the pressure, and the enlargement is noted. This will be understood from the table which records the expansion of a cylinder, No. 2600, tested in August 1868, being 4 inches in length, with an external diameter 1.2500 inch.

Powder Charge.	Diameter after firing each round.	Enlargement after firing each round.
Grains.	Inches.	Inches.
65	1.2588	.0088
150	1.2855	.0267
175	1.3154	.0299
200	1.3464	.0310
225	1.3796	.0332
250	1.4444	.0648
275	Cylinder burst, but remained in one piece.	
Total enlargement after firing 250 grains .1944 in.		

The following illustration shows the cylinder in its various stages :—

1.—Before firing.

2.—After firing a few rounds.

3.—After bursting. The excellence of the metal being proved by the amount of powder used, and its tearing open in one piece.

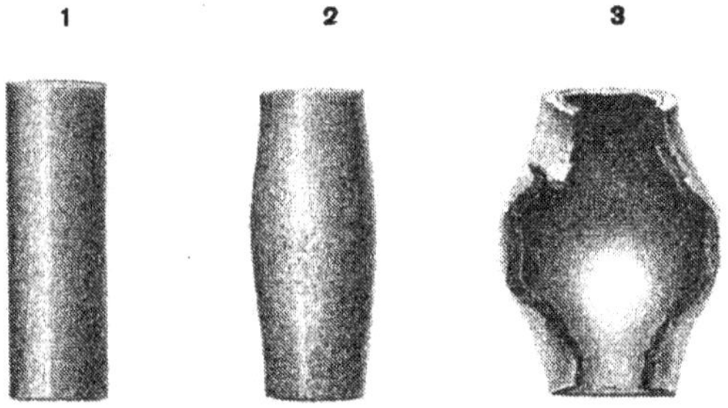

A cylinder test is the only one which will show the strength of different metals in combination, and I have applied it to estimate the strength of a cast-iron converted gun as compared with a similar gun made of sound ductile steel.

A tube was prepared of wrought iron 4 inches long, $\frac{3}{4}$-inch internal diameter, and .066 inch thick ; a cast-iron tube, .184 inch in thickness was fitted over the iron tube, that being the proportion adopted in converting cast-iron 68-pounders into rifled guns for marine artillery.

With a charge of 30 grains of powder the cast-iron shell broke into 14 pieces, and the wrought-iron tube opened out.

In a simple tube of the same dimensions made of fluid-compressed steel, and charged with 30 grains, the tube remained intact, and the enlargement was nil.

EXPERIMENTAL CYLINDERS TESTED BY GUNPOWDER.

The following are the details of experiments, made in order to test the strength of metal cylinders.

The cylinder A is of *fluid-compressed steel*, it is 26 inches in length, 7.83 inches external diameter, and 2.56 inches internal diameter, and further experiments are still to be made with it.

A

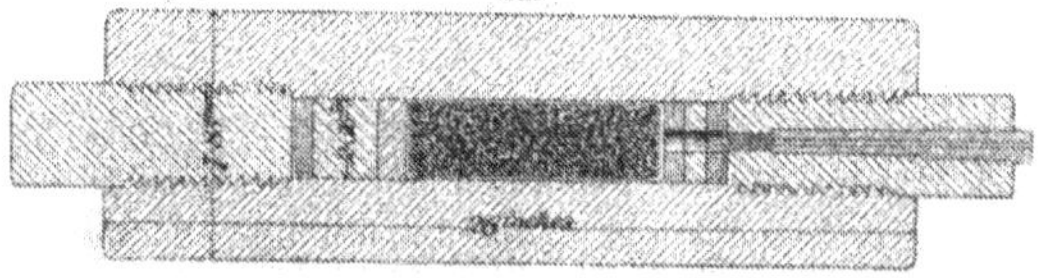

The cylinder is charged with 1¼ lbs. of powder, and it will be seen that there is no escape for the powder gas except through the touch-hole, which is 0.10 of an inch in diameter.

After each discharge the cylinder is carefully measured, and the enlargement of the inside and outside diameters is recorded.

After 48 discharges the enlargement of the inside diameter was .1919 inch, and that of the outside diameter .0485 inch.

During these trials some interesting experiments have been made with different metals for the vent. A copper vent was enlarged by one explosion from one-tenth of an inch to one-fourth of an inch. Experiments have also been made on the compression of different metals by the force of the explosion, from which we shall be able to ascertain the strength of powder, by comparing the results thus obtained with the compression of the same metals by other means.

It most probably would be thought by the readers of the above remarks, that results so striking and so important in a national point of view would have commanded willing attention, at least from those who, occupying official positions, must have been able to appreciate, and were in a manner bound fully to test their value.

It is with regret that I feel compelled to state here that such has not been the case; as an example of the difficulty I have experienced in bringing these matters under the notice of the military advisers of the War Office, I may mention that in November 1869 I exhibited to Mr. Cardwell and Mr. Childers my process of compressing fluid steel. General Lefroy was present, and made an official report on what he saw, in the capacity of professional adviser to the Secretary of State for War. Referring to the experiment of the discharge of powder in a closed steel cylinder, which had been made before him, General Lefroy stated:—

"I think it not improbable that good cast iron would stand the test shown."

Although I was perfectly aware that cast iron is incapable of standing such a test, I, nevertheless (as the opinion of the Director-General is of so much official importance), had a cylinder of precisely the same dimensions made of cast iron, which I knew to be of good quality, and instead of using 1½ lbs. of powder it was charged with 3 ounces.

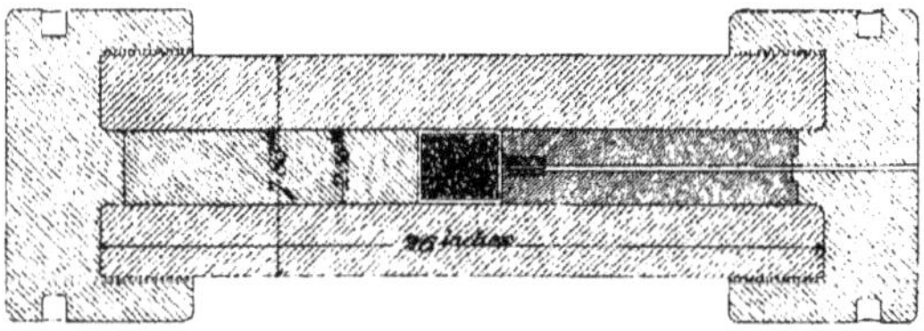

The following was the result:—That whereas the cylinder of my metal is still intact after 48 explosions, each of 1½ lbs. (24 ounces) of powder, the cast-iron cylinder burst into 20 pieces at the first discharge of 3 ounces.

I have also had a cylinder made of cast iron, with a coiled wrought-iron tube inside, to represent the proportions adopted in the conversion of the old 8-inch smooth-bore guns into rifled 64-pounders. The inner diameter or bore was 2.56 inches, the thickness of the wrought-iron tube 0.690 inches, and the outside diameter 7.83 inches.

The area of the cast iron was not sufficient to support the end strain, and the caps were held together by additional screws fitted into an external casing.

Four charges were fired, the weight of powder being 5, 6, 8, and 10 ounces respectively. The enlargement of the cylinder after the discharge of 8 ounces, was .0,317 inches on the inside, and .0,017 inches on the outside. The 4th discharge of only 10 ounces broke the cylinder up into fragments, viz.:—of cast iron 174, and of wrought iron 7 pieces.

These results were quite contrary to the expectation of the Director-General, but were perfectly consistent with my former experiments. I cannot understand how the Director-General could persist in the conversion of cast-iron guns in the face of such proofs of their weakness and inefficiency; and it is difficult to see how such persistence, involving as it does a large expenditure of public money, can be justified.

On the 8th of October, 1872, I exploded, during the trials at Southport, 1½ lbs. of R. L. G. powder in a cylinder made of Whitworth fluid-compressed steel, with no other escape for the gas generated than a vent one-tenth of an inch in diameter.

The cylinder was a copy of the breech end of a 9-pounder Whitworth muzzle-loading gun, cut off at the trunnion, with the projectile screwed in. It is estimated that the consequent strain would be six times greater than that produced if the shot were free to leave the gun.

The drawing shows the cylinder in section.

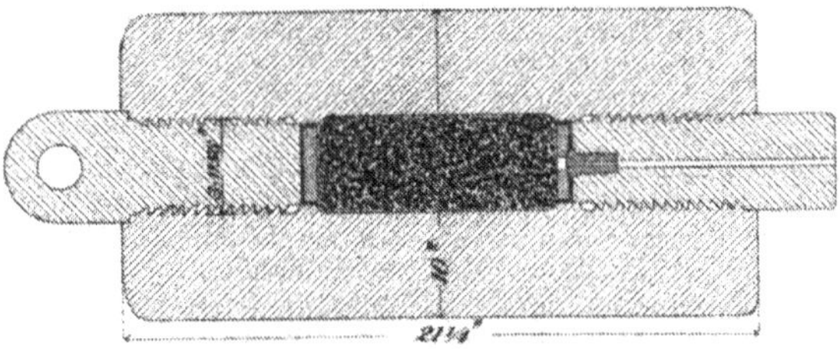

When fired, it recoiled 32 inches along the sand from the rush of gas through the vent, although its weight was 467 lbs. The screwed plug was then taken out, and the cylinder was measured both externally and internally, but no alteration had taken place. The vent, however, had been enlarged in diameter by the rush of the gas from one-tenth to two-tenths of an inch.

Table of Qualities of Steel.

The different strengths and ductilities of steel manufactured at the works of Sir Joseph Whitworth & Co., may be thus tabulated.

For convenience I arrange the metal in four groups, distinguished by the colours Red, Blue, Brown, and Yellow. In each group No. 1 represents the most ductile metal, and the ductility decreases as we pass on to Nos. 2 and 3. The purposes for which the steel is available are given in the table. The average tensile strength of No. 2, Red, is 40 tons per square inch, the ductility being 32 per cent. The tensile strength of No. 2, Blue, is 50 tons, the ductility being 22 per cent. The tensile strength of No. 2, Brown, is 60 tons, the ductility being 17 per cent. The tensile strength of No. 2, Yellow, is 68 tons, the ductility being 10 per cent.

	Tensile Strength per sq. inch.	Per centage of elongation or Ductility.	
No. 1 RED. *No. 2 RED.* *No. 3 RED.*	40 Tons.	32	Axles, Boilers, Connecting Rods, Cross Heads, Crank Pins, Hydraulic Cylinders, Locomotive and Marine Cranks, Propeller Shafts, Rivets, Railway Tyres, Guide Screws, Gun Furniture, Gun Barrels, Air Vessels for Torpedoes, Carriages for Field and Naval Ordnance.
No. 1 BLUE. *No. 2 BLUE.* *No. 3 BLUE.*	48 Tons.	24	Cylinder Linings for Marine Engines, Slide Bars for Locomotives, Shafting, Couplings, large and small Lathe Mandrils, Spindles for Drilling Machines, Eccentric Shafts for Punching and Shearing Machines, Pillars for Hydraulic Presses, large Swages, Pressure Blocks for Rivetting Machines, Hammers, large Hoops and Trunnions for for Ordnance.
No. 1 BROWN. *No. 2 BROWN.* *No. 3 BROWN.*	58 Tons.	17	Large Planing and Lathe Tools, large Shears, Drills, Smiths' Punches and Dies, small Swages, Smiths' Sets, Cold Chisels, Screw Tools, Rollers for Corn Mills, Armour Piercing Shells.
No. 1 YELLOW. *No. 2 YELLOW.* *No. 3 YELLOW.*	68 Tons.	10	Boring Tools, Finishing Tools for Planing and Turning.
SPECIAL ALLOY,	72 Tons.	14	For particular purposes.

NOTE.—In some cases it may be desirable to use Nos. 1 or 3 of each colour; these being of intermediate strength and ductility. Sword Blades would be No. 3 Blue or No. 1 Brown.

No. 1 Red may be used instead of wrought iron, it is very soft and ductile, and entirely free from marks and seams.

CHAPTER II.

In the year 1854, when Lord Hardinge was endeavouring to obtain the best possible rifle with which to arm the British troops, he requested me to aid him by investigating the mechanical principles applicable in the construction of an efficient weapon. I willingly agreed to do so, subject, however, to the condition that I should have a suitable gallery, protected from changes in the wind and from fluctuations in the atmosphere, wherein to carry on the experiments which were necessary for enabling me to arrive at any sound conclusion.

It was absolutely essential to track the path of a rifle bullet throughout its entire course, to determine whether its point preserved a true forward direction, and to record its trajectory. This could be done most readily in a closed gallery provided with screens of very light tissue paper.

Accordingly a gallery, 500 yards in length, was erected in my grounds at Rusholme, in the year 1855. Its height was 20 feet and width 16 feet; it was slated, and had openings on the south side only for the admission of light and for getting rid of the smoke.

The first result of the work done in this gallery was the construction of my small-bore rifle.

First Comparative Trials of the Whitworth and Enfield Rifles.

In the year 1855 I commenced a series of experiments in the new rifle gallery, and was at that time requested to adhere to the service charge of powder, viz., 70 grains, as well as to the service weight of bullet, viz., 530 grains, but I was unrestricted in every other particular.

The barrel of the Enfield rifle, as then used in the service, was 39 inches in length, its bore being .577 of an inch in diameter. The rifling was effected by three spiral grooves, making 1 turn in 78 inches, and the bullet rotated half a turn during its passage along the barrel. The length of the bullet was 1.81 diameters of the bore.

The bullet was cylindro-conoidal ; it was wrapped in paper, and was made of such a size as to pass easily down the barrel, and had a conical wood plug in its hollow base. At the instant of firing, the explosive force of the powder caused the bullet to become expanded or upset, and thus moulded it to fit the grooves in the bore. It was essential that the lead should be very pure and soft in order to allow of its being properly expanded into the grooves.

The bullet is shown in the diagram.

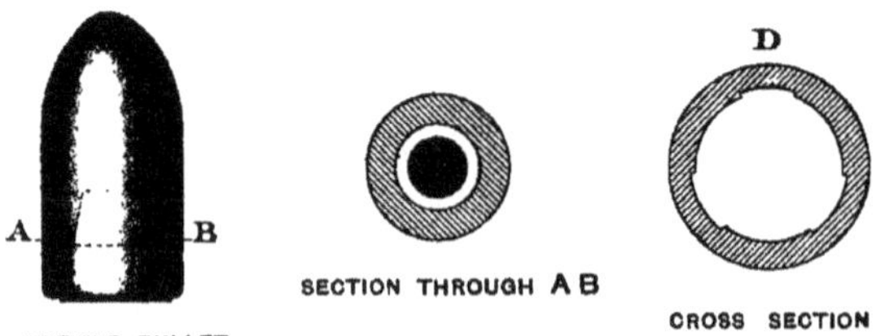

ENFIELD BULLET.

SECTION THROUGH A B

CROSS SECTION OF ENFIELD BARREL.

The cross section of the barrel is given at D, the circular

portions, which do no work in rotating the bullet, are called *lands*, and the grooves run in a screw thread of uniform pitch between the lands.

The barrel of the Whitworth rifle is 39 inches in length, the interior is hexagonal in section, and, instead of consisting partly of non-effective lands and partly of grooves, has rifling surfaces which are wholly effective. The rifling turn is much quicker than that of the Enfield rifle, being 1 turn in 20 inches, and the angular corners of the hexagon are rounded in the manner shown. The maximum diameter of the bore is .490 of an inch, and the minimum diameter is .451 of an inch.

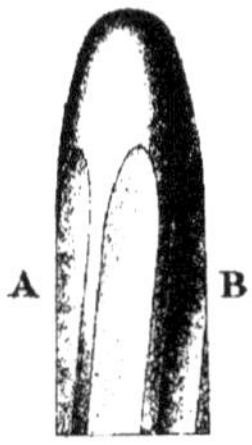

WHITWORTH BULLET.

SECTION THROUGH A B

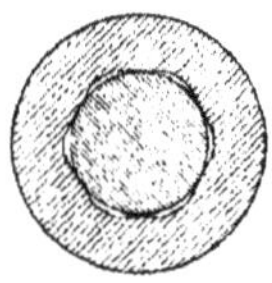

CROSS SECTION OF CYLINDRICAL BULLET IN HEXAGONAL BARREL.

The bullet may be either hexagonal or cylindrical; in the latter case, it will expand and be driven into the recesses of the hexagon, and will adapt itself to the curves of the spiral rifling; in the former case the inclined sides of the hexagon offer no direct resistance to this expansion, which is easily effected. The length of the bullet is 3 diameters of the bore.

With all expanding bullets, a quick burning powder must be employed. The expansion depends on the sudden action of the powder upon a bullet possessing inertia, it therefore fails with a slow burning powder.

If there be a mechanical fit between the bullet and the bore of a muzzle-loading rifle, this expansion is no longer necessary, and the bullet may then be made of alloys of tin and lead of any degree of hardness, or a hardened steel bullet may be used. It is perfectly easy to form a mechanically-fitting bullet adapted to the hexagonal rifling, on account of the simplicity of the form, but quite impracticable to obtain an accurate fit between the bullet and the bore of the rifle where any system of grooves is adopted.

The expansion principle may be combined with an easy mechanical fit, so that a projectile made of metal harder than lead, such as an alloy of lead and tin, may be used, and the bullet will then expand sufficiently to fill the bore, giving a penetration more than double that of lead.

In my earlier experiments I tried the effect of lengthening the bullet of the Enfield rifle, and I showed, by means of a piece of tissue paper placed three yards from the gun, that an increase of only a quarter of an inch in length caused the bullet to strike obliquely. This fact was clearly ascertained by the mark left upon the paper. I then made a barrel of the same bore with a twist of 1 turn in 30 inches, instead of 1 turn in 78 inches, and I kept the weight of the lengthened bullet at 530 grains by making a portion of the interior hollow. The result was that with the same charge the bullet hit the target at the same height.

Having thus proved that there was no loss of range on account of the increased rotation of the bullet, and that the trajectory was as good as before, I made another barrel, reducing the minimum diameter to .5 inch, and lengthening the projectile, and finally I reduced the bore to .45 inch.

In order to satisfy myself as to the effect of increased twist in the rifling, I tried barrels with 1 turn in 20 inches, 1 turn in 10 inches, 1 turn in 5 inches, and lastly with 1 turn in 1 inch. I fired from these barrels mechanically-fitting bullets of lead and tin, and with the barrel rifled to 1 turn in 1 inch (using 35 grains of powder), I penetrated through 7 inches of elm-tree planks.

In this way I exhausted the subject, and arrived at the result that the best twist for a rifled musket bullet would be 1 turn in 20 inches, the minimum diameter of the barrel being .45 inches.

This construction gave the best shooting with the charge of powder and weight of bullet to which I was limited.

If the ordinary strength of a man was greater than it is, the Enfield bore would be right, but it would be necessary to increase the length of bullet and the twist of rifling, the rifle itself being also made heavier in proportion.

I experienced great opposition to the change of rifle turn from 1 turn in 78 inches to 1 turn in 20 inches, or I should have made the twist somewhat more rapid in order to fire a steel bullet when necessary for penetration. It should be understood that the amount of rotation must be increased when the specific gravity of the bullet is made less, otherwise the projectile will fall over in its flight,—that is to say, an iron projectile requires more rotation than one made of lead.

The same principles apply in determining the rotation for the heaviest guns. A long projectile turns over unless it has sufficient rotation, and the twist for field guns should not be less than 1 turn in 15 diameters. The gun will then fire projectiles 6 diameters in length.

I have always contended that the primary element of success in long range shooting, is *length of bullet*, and generally that great range, with a low trajectory, accuracy and penetration are obtained by employing a long bullet, high rotation, and a large powder charge.

The superiority of the Whitworth, as compared with the Enfield rifle, was first proved in a series of trials made at Hythe, in the year 1857, under the direction of Lord Panmure, then Minister of War.

These trials led to no satisfactory conclusion, and after a lapse of eighteen months a Committee of Officers reported to the Government in 1859 that the *bore* of my rifle *was to small for use as a military weapon.*

Compare with this the report of another Committee of Officers made in 1862, "*that the makers of every small-bore rifle, having any pretensions to special accuracy, have copied to the letter the three main elements of success adopted by Mr. Whitworth, viz., diameter of bore, degree of spiral, and large proportion of rifling surface.*"

In 1869 a Special Committee reported to the War Office that *the calibre of a breech-loading rifle, should be .45 inches, as appearing to be the most suitable for a military arm.* This conclusion is directly contrary to that arrived at in 1859, but is the exact *bore* which I recommended in 1857.

The mechanical question is the same whether we deal with a rifled musket or the heaviest gun. I have from the commencement advocated one uniform system, the value of which I have established by direct experiment.

As regards heavy artillery, it will probably require some long interval before the professional advisers will be enabled to see that sound ductile steel is the best material for a gun, that the bore for a given weight of gun should be made smaller than that used in the service, that the projectile should be lengthened, that its rotation should be increased, and that the stud system should be abolished.

In this direction they have made one step. They have taken the weight I proposed for a gun of 12 inches bore, and have increased the weight of the service 12-inch gun from 25 to 35 tons. In all other respects the Woolwich system is in direct opposition to my own. Following past precedent it must be expected that when the truths I have endeavoured to press upon official attention are fully understood, and action is taken upon them, my part in first developing them will probably be forgotten.

Rifle Trials at Hythe in 1857.

The peculiar features of the Whitworth rifle may be summed up as follows :—

1.—The bore is much smaller than that of the Enfield rifle.

Whitworth ...	Maximum diameter ...	.49-inch.
	Minimum diameter ...	.45 „
Enfield.........	Maximum diameter ...	.61 „
	Minimum diameter ...	.577 „

2.—The length of the bullet is increased.

Whitworth—length 3 diameters.

Enfield—length 1.81 diameters.

3.—The twist of the rifling is increased.

Whitworth—1 turn in 20 inches.

Enfield—1 turn in 78 inches.

4.—The form of the Whitworth bore is polygonal, being a hexagon with the edges rounded.

The form of the Enfield bore is cylindrical, with grooves and lands.

The Government were desirous of testing the merits of my new arm, and of comparing it with the Enfield rifle, and a series of trials were made by the direction of Lord Panmure. The subjoined account of these trials, is extracted from the "*Times*," of April 23rd, 1857 :—

For the last few days a very interesting and important series of experiments has been in progress at the Government School of Musketry, Hythe, in order to test the comparative merits of the Whitworth and Enfield rifles. The trial, which was of a most searching and impartial character, was conducted by Colonel Hay, the able head of the school, and has terminated in establishing beyond all doubt the great and decided superiority of Mr. Whitworth's invention. The Enfield rifle, which was considered so much better than any other, has been completely beaten. In accuracy of fire, in penetration, and in range its rival excels it to a degree which hardly leaves room for comparison.

The following table gives the best results that have been obtained from 10 shots of each arm respectively in the course of the experiments, which were brought to a close yesterday, in the presence of Lord Panmure, and of a number of military and scientific spectators :—

Rifle.	Range Yards.	Elevation Degrees.	Figure of Merit.*
			Feet.
Whitworth...	500	1 .1	0.37
Enfield	"	1.32	2.24
Whitworth...	800	2.22	1.0
Enfield	"	2.45	4.11
Whitworth...	1,100	3.45	2.41
Enfield	"	4.12	8.04
Whitworth...	1,400	5.0	4.62
Enfield	"	6.20 to 7.0	No hits.
Whitworth...	1,800	6.40	11.62
Enfield	"	——	——

It would appear from these figures that at 500 yards, in 10 shots, the Manchester rifle has a superior accuracy of 1·87 of a foot; at 800 yards 3·11; at 1,100 yards 5·63; and that at 1,400 yards and upwards, the

* The *figure of merit* is the average divergence of the number of shots fired.

Enfield weapon ceases to afford any data for comparison. In penetration the results have been equally decisive; the Whitworth projectile with the regulation charge of powder going through 33 half-inch planks of elm, and being brought up by a solid bulk beyond, while the Enfield ball could not get past the 13th plank.

All these were made by firing from a beautifully constructed machine rest, which placed both weapons on a footing of perfect equality, as to the other conditions under which they were tested.

By referring to the table of experiments it will be seen that the target made by the former weapon at 1,100 yards is nearly as good as that made by the latter at 500 yards. These are great results to have achieved, and amply justify the forethought of the late Lord Hardinge in securing the services of so eminent a mechanic as Mr. Whitworth for the improvement of the rifle. Until he took the subject in hand, the proper principles for guidance in the construction of the weapon had not been accurately determined.

General Hay informed me that the best figure of merit obtained by any rifle at a range of 500 yards, before the year 1857, was 24 inches, and here the new Whitworth rifle had a figure of merit of 12 inches at 800 yards, and of 4.62 feet at 1,400 yards. The figures of its competitor, the Enfield rifle, at the same ranges were 4.11 feet and "*no hits*," that is to say, the Enfield bullet could not touch a target, 14 feet square, at 1,400 yards range.

The accuracy of the Whitworth rifle may be estimated from the following facts, a figure of merit of 10½ inches has been obtained at a range of 1,000 yards, 20 shots being fired. At a range of 500 yards it is a common thing to obtain a mean deviation of 3 to 5 inches, from my mechanical rest in the gallery, with 20 shots.

Trials of the Whitworth and Enfield Rifles, made at Woolwich in the Year 1857.

After the contest at Hythe, a series of experiments were conducted by a Committee appointed by the Minister of War, and the enquiries were especially directed to these points :—

(1) Precision, (2) penetration, (3) range.

The trials were made in July and August, 1857, and the best results obtained from the Whitworth and Enfield rifles were officially reported to be the following :—

Rifle.	Range.	Figure of Merit.
Whitworth	500 yds.	10.194
Enfield ...	500 „	18.240
Whitworth	800 „	18.264
Enfield ...	800 „	45.750
Whitworth	1,400 „	74.844
Enfield ...	1,400 „	110.451
Whitworth	1,700 „	129.762
Enfield ...	1,700 „	beyond range.
Whitworth	2,000 „	129.565
Enfield ...	2,000 „	beyond range.

In the experiment on penetration, a Whitworth bullet made of a hard alloy passed through 34 half-inch elm boards, while a tubular bullet passed through 34 of the same boards, cutting out clean cores in its passage. The range was 307 yards.

I have not any record of the penetration of the Enfield bullet, except that given in the Hythe trials, where it passed through 12 half-inch elm planks, and was stopped by the 13th plank.

A Rifle Fired by the Queen.

The first prize meeting of the National Rifle Association was held at Wimbledon on the 2nd July, 1860. Her Majesty, the Queen, graciously signified her intention of inaugurating it in person, and also of firing the first rifle shot.

Accordingly a Whitworth rifle was mounted on the mechanical rest, which is dependent on the use of my true planes for its geometrical exactness. The drawing shows the rest supported on a tripod stand, and weighted to ensure steadiness; the rifle is placed on a light steel slide, having true plane surfaces sliding on other true planes, which construction ensures that the recoil of the piece shall take place in one definite

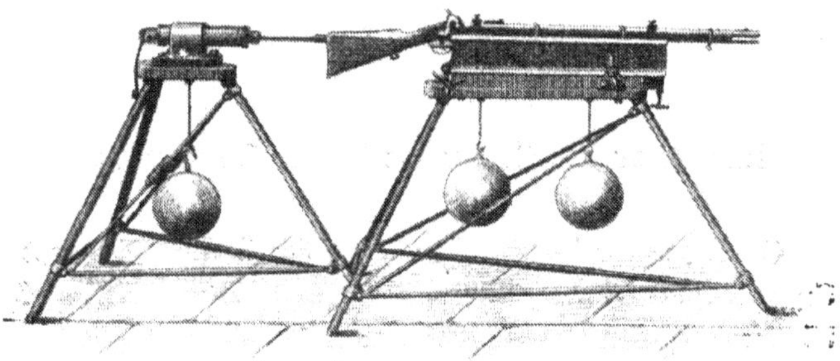

unchangeable line. Nothing can disturb the accuracy of the aim at the instant of firing.

A spring balance fixed on a smaller tripod, also weighted, receives the recoil by means of a projecting arm, and measures its amount.

The target having been fixed at a distance of 400 yards, a silken cord attached to the trigger was handed to Her Majesty by me, and the rifle was discharged by a slight pull on the cord.

The adjustment was so accurate that the bullet struck the target within 1¼ inches from the centre, or point of intersection of the two cross lines, as shown by the diagram copied from a photograph :—

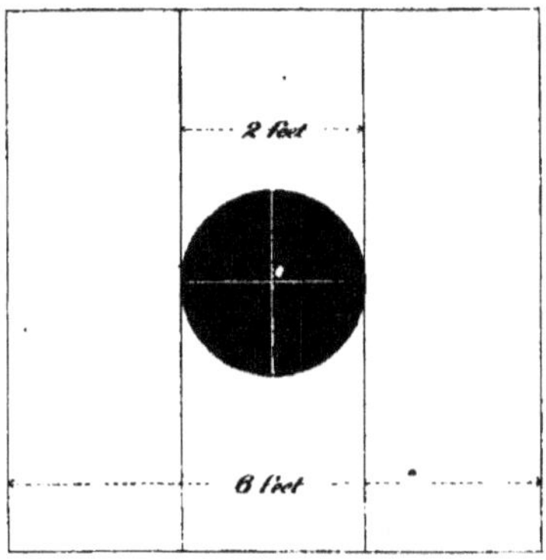

Report by the Ordnance Select Committee.

On the 26th of November, 1862, the Ordnance Select Committee published the following results of a series of trials made with the Whitworth and Enfield rifles.

The dimensions and constructions of the two rifles are stated below, the mean angle of elevation for a given range is tabulated, and also the mean radial deviation or figure of merit. The experiments were instituted by the Secretary of State for War in the year 1861.

ENFIELD :—
Diameter of bore ... 0.577in.
Pitch of rifling, 1 turn in 87ins.
No. of grooves 3

WHITWORTH :—
Diameter across angles, .490in.
" " flats, 0.451in.
Pitch of rifling, 1 turn in 20ins.
No. of grooves ... ... Hexagon.

	ENFIELD.		WHITWORTH.	
Range Yards.	Mean Radial Deviation.	Mean Angle.	Mean Radial Deviation.	Mean Angle.
	Inches.		Inches.	
300	12.69	0° 44′ 8″	3.86	0° 56′ 49″
500	19.80	1° 45′ 13″	7.29	1° 23′ 37″
800	41.61	2° 46′ 6″	15.67	2° 17′ 6″
1,000	95.01	4° 3′ 33″	23.13	3° 5′ 36″
1,200	133.53	5° 9′ 48″	46.92	4° 3′ 6″

THE HENRY AND METFORD RIFLES.

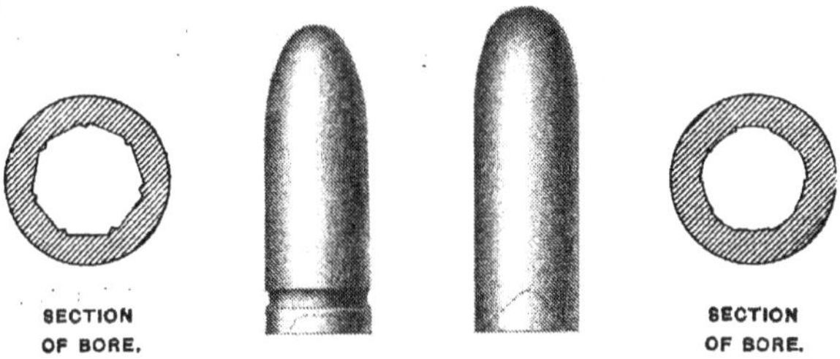

SECTION OF BORE. HENRY. METFORD. SECTION OF BORE.

I here confine myself to pointing out the manner in which my system has been followed in the construction of the Henry and Metford rifles. The drawing shows in section the bore of each gun, as well as the respective bullets.

The Henry rifle has a polygonal bore with seven instead of six sides.

The diameter of a circle touching each flat side of the polygon is .45 of an inch; the maximum diameter of the grooving is .457 of an inch.

The bullet is 2.93 diameters in length.

The twist of the rifling is 1 turn in 22 inches.

When the bullet moulds itself to the form of the rifling, each angular point is cut away by the seven projecting sharp edges which protrude in the barrel at the junction of the sides of the polygon.

This alteration in the rifling of my barrel was no doubt done in order to meet the requirements of a cylindrical hardened lead bullet, which cannot be much upset by the powder. It may be very well for match shooting when in good order. The difference between the maximum and minimum diameters is small, and the amount of upsetting required by the bullet is proportionately less; but the use of a steel bullet is rendered impracticable, and the rifling is unsuited for the great wear and tear of a military weapon.

Regarded as a military arm, the additions to my barrel above referred to have nullified its efficiency.

I was the first to use a hardened bullet, but I made it the shape of the barrel, and obtained a mechanical fit, which enabled me to use a steel or any other hardened bullet. On the importance of being able to use a steel bullet, I would refer to Sir John Burgoyne's letter of December the 11th, 1857, quoted in the appendix.

The alteration of the twist from 1 turn in 20 inches to 1 turn in 22 inches, must have been made purely for the sake of alteration. I had found it requisite to go from 1 turn in 78 inches of the Enfield to 1 turn in 20 inches. If the steel bullet is to be considered a matter of importance, I should prefer 1 turn in 17 inches, because steel requires a higher rotation than lead on account of its less specific gravity.

The Metford rifle has a bore of a cylindrical character. It is made up of a series of cylindrical portions concentric with the axis of the bore, and alternating in size. This provides a series of grooves, five in number, and cylindrical in section, with sharp sloping edges.

The maximum diameter is .47 of an inch, the minimum diameter being .462 of an inch.

The bullet is 3.02 diameters in length.

The barrel is rifled with an increasing twist, commencing at the breech end with 1 turn in 48 inches, and terminating at the muzzle with 1 turn in 16 inches.

It will be remembered that in the Whitworth rifle the bore is hexagonal, the mean diameter is .47 of an inch, the bullet is 3 diameters in length, and the twist of the rifling is 1 turn in 20 inches.

Hexagonal Rifling.

I have stated that the form of the bore of the Whitworth rifle is polygonal, being a hexagon with rounded edges; it is therefore a combination of a straight line and a circle, and its surfaces are those most easily produced in the workshop.

There is a geometrical simplicity pertaining to the polygonal form which is unattainable by any other form.

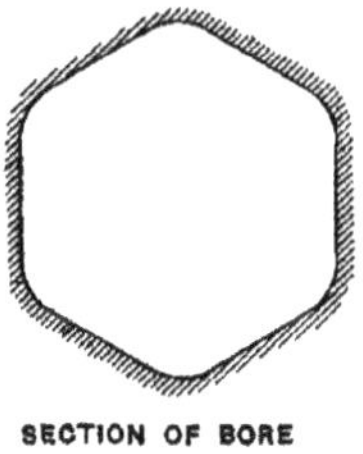

SECTION OF BORE

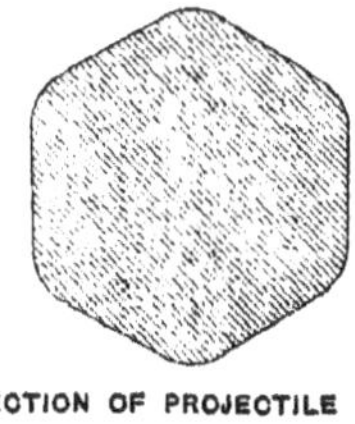

SECTION OF PROJECTILE

The amount of bearing surface for giving rotation, and which also conduces to the centreing of the shot, ***depends upon the difference*** between the maximum and minimum diameters of the bore; this difference, in fact, represents the hold which the barrel has upon the projectile. In any grooved system of rifling you pass more rapidly from the maximum to the minimum diameter, and the extent of bearing surface is *diminished* accordingly, whereas in the hexagonal system, there is a long inclined bearing surface, the section of which is a straight line starting from the minimum diameter and running into a circle at the end of the maximum diameter.

A polygonal rifled projectile is applicable to the largest cannon as well as to small arms, and I have adopted the hexagonal form, because it gives me the best working difference between the maximum and minimum diameters.

It will be observed that the hexagonal form of the projectile is analogous to that of the hexagonal nut universally used.

It may be said that this record of my experiments, showing how the modern rifle has become what it is in range, in penetration, and in accuracy, has ceased to be of interest or importance since the new element of rapid firing has been brought to bear with such important results by the introduction of breech loading. I would state in reply that breech loading and rapid fire give increased importance and value to range, penetration, and accuracy, as the primary and essential qualities of the rifle. However necessary these qualities may have been for the muzzle loader, they are still more requisite with an arm which must otherwise waste its ammunition. Rapid firing must rest on the very best system of rifling, as its only safe basis.

The Form of Projectiles for Flight.

I have long since worked out the question of the form of projectiles. The earlier experiments were made with the 1-pounder field gun, at Manchester, and the results of my experience may be thus stated.

FIG. 1.

TAPER REAR.

FIG. 2.

PARALLEL REAR.

The best form for flight (which gives the longest range with the lowest trajectory) has the head shaped to a curve of least resistance, with a tapered rear, and is from 3 to 4 diameters long. (Fig. 1).

In another form of projectile the head is the same, but the rear has parallel sides. This is a better form for a shell, as the projectile holds a greater bursting charge of powder. (Fig. 2).

The projectile with tapered rears is the best for flight in all cases, but the increase of range produced by the taper is not important at low elevations. The advantage increases in proportion to the elevation. In the longest ranges a shot with a taper rear will range upwards of a mile further than one that is parallel; it is, therefore, very desirable to use it for long ranges.

No alteration of this form can be made without producing an inferior result.

Trials for Range and Accuracy at Southport in 1860.

The advisers of the Government have been in full possession of the results obtained from time to time with guns made on my system. There have been trials almost without number, and the subjoined tables show what was done in February 1860, at Southport, in the presence of General Sir John Burgoyne, Captain the Hon. G. Wrottesley, Colonel Campbell (representing the Ordnance Select Committee), and other officers.

The trials were made with 3, 12, and 80-pounder breech-loading guns.

1.—With the 3-pounder gun, nine rounds being fired at an elevation of 3°, with a powder charge of 7½ oz.

Mean range in yards	1,582	Mean deflection in feet ...	1.5 right	
Mean variation in range ...	10.8	Mean variation in deflection	1.5	

2.—Ten rounds fired from the same gun at an elevation of 10°, with a powder charge of 7½ oz.

Mean range in yards	3,842	Mean deflection in feet ...	27.8 right	
Mean variation in range ...	42.3	Mean variation in deflection	9.6	

3.—Eight rounds fired from the same gun at an elevation of 20°, with a powder charge of 8½ oz.

Mean range in yards	6,671	Mean deflection in feet ...	46 right	
Mean variation in range ...	47	Mean variation in deflection	12.3	

4.—Five rounds fired from the same gun at an elevation of 35°, with a powder charge of 9½ oz.

Mean range in yards	9,580	Mean deflection in feet ...	169 right	
Mean variation in range ...	81.6	Mean variation in deflection	57.8	

5.—With the 12-pounder gun, ten rounds being fired at an elevation of 5°, with a powder charge of 2 lbs.

Mean range in yards	2,336	Mean deflection in feet ...	8 right	
Mean variation in range ...	16.2	Mean variation in deflection	3.1	

6.—Four rounds fired from the same gun at an elevation of 7°, with a powder charge of 2 lbs.

Mean range in yards	3,098	Mean deflection in feet ...	.75 right	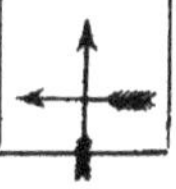
Mean variation in range ...	9.5	Mean variation in deflection	1.62	

7.—With the 80-pounder gun, four rounds being fired at an elevation of 7°, with a powder charge of 14 lbs.

Mean range in yards	3,492	Mean deflection in feet ...	17.5 right	
Mean variation in range ...	8	Mean variation in deflection	1.75	

Trials for Range and Accuracy at Shoeburyness in 1868.

These trials were made by the Ordnance Select Committee, and the object was to compare the ranges obtained from a 9-inch Whitworth muzzle-loading gun, with projectiles weighing 250 lbs. and 310 lbs. respectively.

The small amount of deflection is well worthy of notice, *and the range of 11,243 yards has never been obtained by any other gun, whatever its form or calibre.*

The details are given in the table annexed :—

Date 1868	Round.	Eleva-tion.	Charge. Lbs.	Projectile.	Range. Yards.	Deflection. Yards.	Wind.	Time of Flight.
Nov.							Moderate.	
20	1	10°	50 tublr.	310 shell.	4,868	1 left.		13.5 sec.
„	2	10°	50 „	250 shot.	5,196	7 right.		14.2 „
„	3	10°	50 solid.	310 shell.	4,021	$6\frac{1}{2}$ „		12.1 „
„	4	33°	50 tublr.	250 shot.	10,300	3 to 400 yds. to the right of line.	Fresh.	not seen.
21	5	33°	50 „	250 „	*11,243*			„
„	6	33°	50 „	310 shell.	11,075			„
„	7	33° 5′	50 „	310 shot.	11,127			„

The weight of the gun was 14 tons 8 cwt.; the bore was hexagonal, the pitch of the rifling being 1 turn in 165 inches. The length of the bore was 140.6 inches, the major diameter being 9.05 inches, and the minor diameter 8.20 inches. The length of the 250 lb. shot was 24.5 inches, and that of the 310 lb. shot was 31.6 inches. The powder charge was 50 lbs., the quality of powder being R.L.G.

After these seven rounds had been fired the gun was measured to the ten-thousandth of an inch, and the measurement compared with that made before the trial. In some parts of the bore, viz., at 30 and 32 inches from the breech, there was no enlargement at all, in others, as at distances of 10, 12, 18, 20, 28, 34, and 38 inches, the enlargement varied from $\frac{1}{10000}$th to $\frac{3}{10000}$ths of an inch. At 2 inches from the breech the enlargement was $\frac{6}{10000}$ths of an inch. At 4, 6, and 8 inches it was $\frac{5}{10000}$ths of an inch, and the greatest enlargement was at 20 and 24 inches, where it amounted to $\frac{7}{10000}$ths of an inch. This was the maximum enlargement after the gun had put forth the prodigious power required to throw 250 pounds weight of metal a distance of nearly 6½ miles.

There were present at this trial, General Lefroy, President of the Ordnance Select Committee; Col. Elwyn, Col. Gordon, Col. Curtis, Lieut. Jones, Captain Noble, Mr. Whitworth, and Captain Donnelly.

In December 1868 there were some further trials of the same gun. The table shows the range and precision :—

Date 1868.	Round.	Elevation.	Charge. Lbs.	Projectile. Weight Kind.	Range. Yards.	Deflection. Yards.	Wind.	Time of Flight.
Dec.	1	10°	40 tublr.	310 shell.	4,650	1.6 right	Very strong.	13.1 sec.
11	2	„	40 „	310 „	4,602	2.6 „		13.1 „
„	3	„	40 „	250 shot.	4,547	3.0 „		13.0 „
„	4	„	40 „	250 „	4,978	7.8 left.		13.9 „
„	5	„	50 „	310 shell.	5,066	12.0 „		13.8 „
„	6	„	50 „	310 „	5,131	1.6 „		13.9 „
„	7	„	50 „	250 shot.	5,426	3.0 „		14.5 „
„	8	„	50 „	250 „	5,480	11.2 „	Lighter.	14.5 „
„	9	„	50 solid.	310 shell.	4,438	6.0 right		12.7 „
„	10	„	50 „	310 „	4,206	7.0 „		12.3 „

To prove the accuracy of the fire of the same gun at smaller ranges, it may be well to record some later experiments made at Shoeburyness, on the 5th of May 1870. Here one shot, weighing 315½ lbs., kept the exact line in a range of about half-a-mile, and another only deviated 7 inches in a nearly equal range, the angle of elevation being 1°.

Five rounds solid shot; length, 24½ inches, windage, .045 inch flats; .071 inch corners.

Charge of powder, 50 lbs. Angle of elevation, 1°.

Round.	Weight of Projectile.	Length of Cartridge.	Recoil. ft. in.	Range. Yards.	Deflection. Yards.	Time of Flight.	Wind.
11	318 lbs.	27½ in.	5 8¾	914	1.2 R.	2.1	Light.
12	320 lbs.	27½ in.	5 8	820	0.2	1.9	
13	321½ lbs.	27¼ in.	5 6½	822	0.8	1.7	
14	315½ lbs.	27½ in.	5 7½	864	Line.	2.0	
15	319½ lbs.	27½ in.	5 8	825	1.2	1.8	

Trial at Southport in 1871.

The range of the Whitworth 12-pounder breech-loading gun was tested at Southport in July 1871.

The powder charge was 4¼ lbs. of R. L. G., and the projectiles were solid shot, 4 diameters in length, tapered at the rear, and weighing 17¼ lbs.

The angle of elevation was 33°, and the ranges obtained by two consecutive shots were 10,856 yards and 10,772 yards respectively, the difference of deflection being only 6 yards. The range of 10,856 yards is 6 miles, 296 yards.

The Form of Projectiles for Penetration.

The best form for penetration is a projectile with a flat head.

I have proved, by a great number of experiments, that a projectile of this form will penetrate armour plates, even when striking obliquely at extreme angles. When constructed as a shell it may be 5 or 6 diameters long, and will have a large internal capacity for holding bursting charges of powder.

When a projectile is designed to penetrate vessels below the water line, it must have a flattened head. No other form is admissible for penetration under water.

This subject of the penetration of a rifled projectile will be better understood if the details of an actual experiment, made in August 1868, are given.

The iron plate shown in the sketch was immersed vertically in water, and the point aimed at was at a depth of 10 inches below the surface.

The gun employed was a 1-pounder; it was laid at an angle of depression of 7° 7′ below the horizontal line, and the length of the path in the water, viz., A B, was 80 inches.

The projectiles fired were rifled, and varied chiefly in the shape of the head; they are shown in the diagram, and are numbered 1, 2, and 3.

The projectiles marked No. 1 were of Whitworth steel, and had flat heads. They passed as nearly as possible in a straight line through the water, striking the target at the points marked 1, 1.

The No. 2 projectiles were deflected upwards, and struck the target just below the water line, at the points marked 2, 2.

The No. 3 projectiles were of white cast iron, chilled in the manner advocated by Major Palliser, and the points struck, marked 3, 3, were 9 inches above the water line.

The drawing shows the exact path taken by one of the

No. 3 projectiles; the screens, placed at equal distances of 20 inches, were perforated in the points C, D, and E, the projectile finally striking the target at the point F. The resistance of the water speedily deflected the projectile upwards, and it was powerless for the purpose of penetration even at the very moderate depth of 10 inches.

This is a perfect demonstration of the influence of the form of the head on penetration.

SECTION OF WATER TANK, SHOWING THE PATH OF No. 3 PROJECTILE.

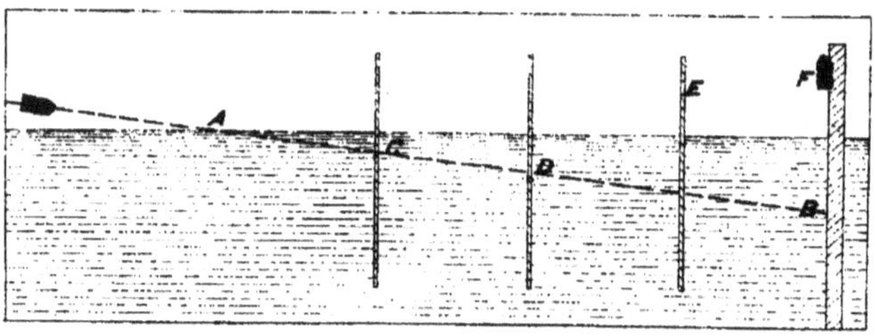

FIG. 1.

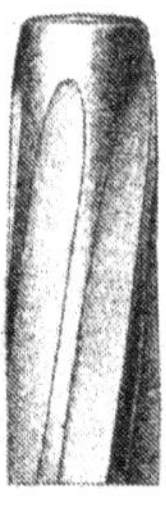

FIG. 2.

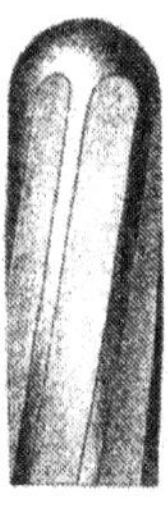

FIG. 3.

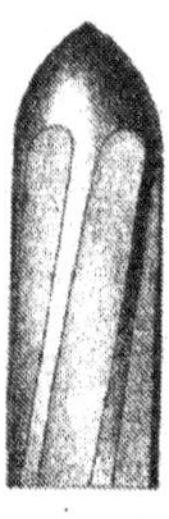

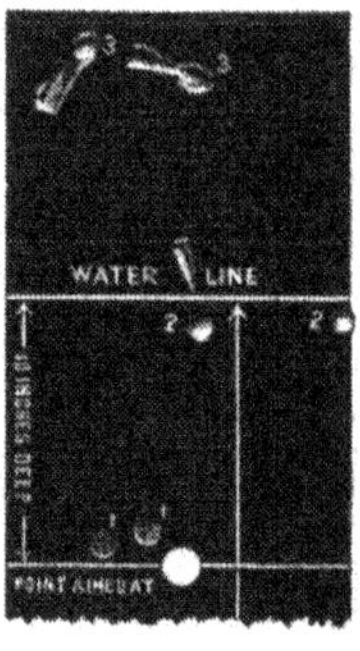

The importance of the subject of penetration of armour-plated ships below the water line appears to have been entirely disregarded. The experiments which I commenced in 1857, and have since made, taken with the enormous penetration given by my breech-loading gun with its increased powder chamber and shell, 5 diameters long, prove that ships are vulnerable below the water line, and that a narrow strip of armour extending a little below that line, does not afford the security which has hitherto been attributed to it.

At the present time our ships of war and coast batteries are provided only with pointed shot, flat-headed projectiles not being admitted into the service. This mistake of adopting a wrong form of projectile has deprived the guns now in use of a very large portion of their power of injuring an enemy.

Experiments on Penetration with Flat-headed Projectiles.

In November 1857, an hexagonally rifled brass gun, being a 24-pound howitzer, was sent to Portsmouth, and subjected to a trial on board the Excellent.

An official report of this trial was addressed by Captain Hewlett, R.N., to Admiral Sir G. F. Seymour, and gave the particulars of the results obtained in penetration under water by a flat-headed projectile.

The gun was laid at a depression of 7°, the shot passed through a wooden butt, made of timber, 8 inches thick, and through water and soft mud up to 53 feet. The penetration varied in the trials, but the greatest amount was that stated.

In October 1858, a 68-pounder cast-iron gun, rifled hexagonally, was fired at Portsmouth from the deck of the Stork gun-boat, at a wrought plate 4 inches thick, attached to the side of the Alfred. The projectile was flat headed, the powder charge was 12 lbs., and the range was 450 yards.

The fourth shot was driven through the plate and entered the planking of the ship's side. *This was the first instance of penetration against a 4-inch armour plate with solid shot,* and from it dates the use of steel projectiles for that purpose.

On the 26th of May, 1860, an 80-lbs. breech-loader was tried at the Nore, in the presence of the Lords of the Admiralty, against the "Trusty" floating battery.

The gun was placed on board the "Carnation" gun-boat, moored at a distance of 200 yards from the "Trusty," and was served with charges of 12 lbs. and 14 lbs. of powder. Only 4 shots were fired, every one of which penetrated the armour plate, two of them passing through the wooden side of the vessel. The Duke of Somerset was afraid that the ship would be sunk and stopped the experiments.

On the 16th of September, 1862, a Whitworth 12-pounder breech-loading gun sent a shot and a shell through a 2½-inch iron plate at 200 yards. A Whitworth 70-pounder muzzle-loading gun was also

BOX MADE OF 4 INCHES OF IRON WITH 9 INCHES OF WOOD IN THE FRONT, FASTENED BY 2½ INCHES OF WOOD TO A BACK COMPOSED OF 2 INCHES OF IRON AND 4 INCHES OF WOOD: THE WHOLE CLAMPED TOGETHER BY IRON.

fired at the same range and sent a shell through a 4-inch iron plate and 9 inches of oak; arranged in the form of a box as shown in the illustration.

The projectile passed completely through the iron plate and front of box, and exploded in the interior of the structure. The box was broken up and destroyed in the manner exhibited in the drawing, which is copied from a photograph. *These were the first experiments on penetration made with steel shells.*

BOX MADE OF 4 INCHES OF IRON, &C., BLOWN TO PIECES BY A STEEL FLAT-HEADED 70-POUNDER WHITWORTH SHELL. RANGE 200 YARDS.

On the 25th of September, 1862, a Whitworth 7-inch muzzle-loading gun sent a shot through a $4\frac{1}{2}$-inch iron plate and 18 inches of teak backing at 600 yards. The trials here referred to were made at Shoeburyness.

In November 1862, some trials were conducted at Shoeburyness with Whitworth guns of 7-inch and $5\frac{1}{2}$-inch bores. The target was constructed of three iron plates, the upper one being $4\frac{1}{2}$ inches thick, and the centre and lower ones being each 5 inches in thickness. The plates were backed with 18 inches of teak, and an external skin of iron, made of $\frac{5}{8}$-inch plate, the whole forming an imitation of a portion of the side of the Warrior ironclad.

The projectiles were 3 diameters in length, flat headed, and made of steel.

The 7-inch shell had a bursting charge of 5 lbs., and weighed 150 lbs. The powder charge of the gun was 27 lbs.

The first round fired was a 7-inch shell at a range of 800 yards. The shell struck the upper or $4\frac{1}{2}$-inch plate and passed through, *exploding in the timber backing.*

The second, third, and fourth shots penetrated the 5-inch plate, *and also burst in the timber backing.* All these shells broke through the inner skin of iron, and it was found on subsequently taking the target to pieces, that 16 timbers were ruined by the firing.

The $5\frac{1}{2}$-inch shells were fired at a range of 600 yards. Each shell weighed 70 lbs., and the powder charge was 13 lbs.

The first and third shots pierced the $4\frac{1}{2}$-inch plate, *and burst in the timber at the back,* but did not penetrate the iron skin.

Four rounds were then fired at the same oak target, armed with an iron plate 6 inches in thickness.

The first and second rounds were fired with ogival-headed steel shells, weighing $136\frac{1}{2}$ lbs. and $135\frac{1}{2}$ lbs. Both shells pierced the target and burst on quitting it.

The third round was fired with a solid shot of hard cast iron, having an ogival head, and weighing 152 lbs. This projectile pierced the target and broke up into fragments.

The fourth round was fired with a flat-headed steel shell weighing 138½ lbs. This penetrated the plate and burst in the wood backing.

On the Penetration of Armour Plates by Long Shells Striking Obliquely.

The experiments to which I now refer were made at Manchester, in the year 1869, and formed the subject matter of a paper read before the British Association at Exeter.

The gun from which the projectiles were fired is called a 3-pounder, though capable of firing much heavier projectiles. It weighs 315 lbs., and the maximum diameter of its bore is 1.85 inch. The charge of powder used, in all cases, was 10 oz., and the weight of the 6-diameter projectile was 6 lbs., the range being 10 yards.

No. 1 is a portion of a plate 2 inches thick, penetrated at an angle of 35°.

No. 2 is a similar piece of plate, 1.7 inch thick, completely penetrated at an angle of 45° by the flat-headed projectile, which buried itself to a depth of 30 inches in a backing of iron borings.

"WHITWORTH" FLAT-HEADED SHELLS, 6 DIAMETERS LONG,

CONTAINING LARGE BURSTING CHARGES.

No. 1.

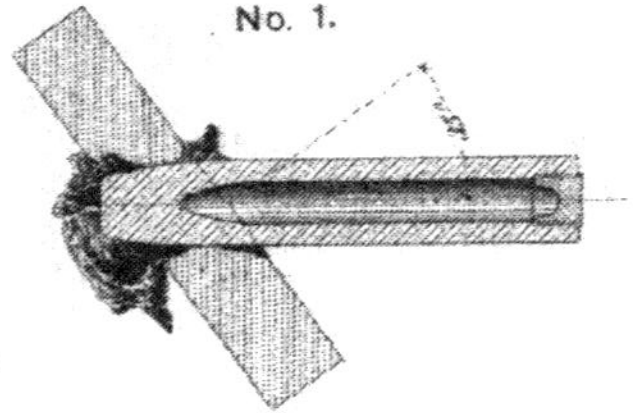

No. 2.

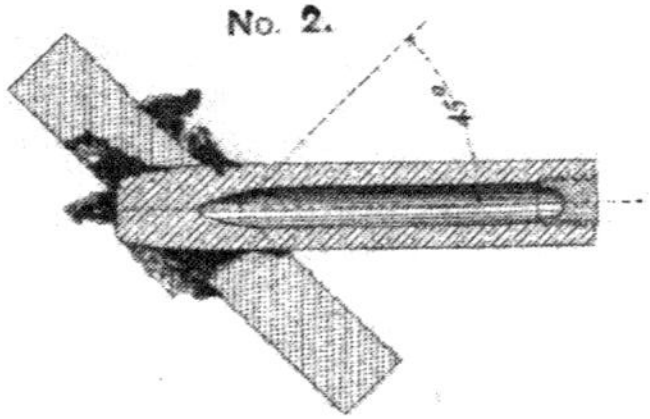

No. 3.

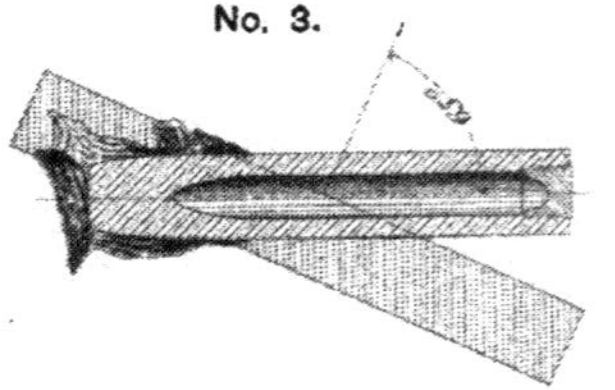

No. 4.
FLAT-HEADED SHOT.
3½ Diams.

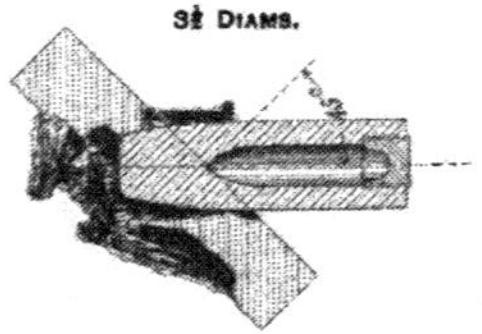

No. 5.
POINTED SOLID SHOT.
3½ Diams.

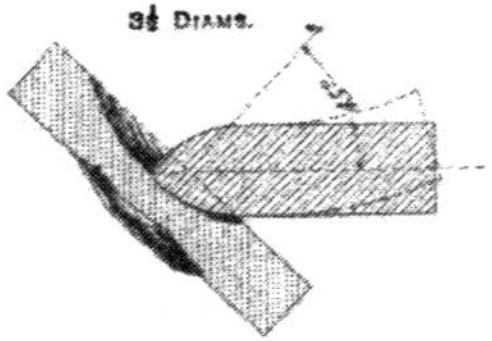

No. 6.
POINTED SOLID SHOT.
2½ Diams.

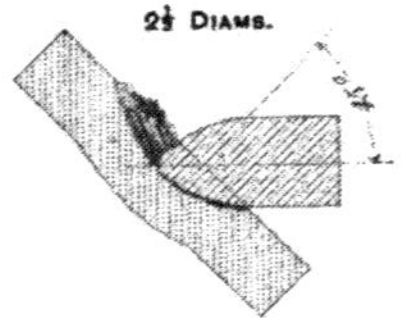

Nos. 1, 2, 3, 4, and 5 were made of "Whitworth" Metal; No. 6 of Pontypool White Iron.

No. 3 is a piece of plate 1.75 inch thick, penetrated at an angle of 65° by the flat-headed projectile.

No. 4 is a plate 1.7 inch thick, nearly penetrated at an angle of 45° by the 3½-diameter flat-headed projectile No. 4.

No. 5 is a plate 1½ inch thick, against which the ogival-pointed projectile was fired at an angle of 45°. The projectile failed to penetrate the plate, being deflected in consequence of the pointed form of the head. The distortion of its shape, given by the dotted lines, indicates the force with which it struck the plate, as well as the good quality of the material which could resist such a test.

No. 6 also is a plate also 1½ inch thick, against which an ogival-pointed service projectile, 2¼ diameters long, made of Pontypool white iron, has been fired: the projectile scooped out a furrow 4 inches long and $\frac{7}{10}$-inch deep, and broke up into fragments, of which 48 were recovered.

The plates Nos. 1 and 3 were made of a thickness such that the projectiles could not quite pass through them, in order that the "work" of the projectiles might be as severe as possible. The data thus obtained fully establish the superiority claimed for the flat-headed projectiles made of fluid-compressed steel, and satisfactorily prove :—

1.—That the flat-headed form is capable of piercing armour plates at extreme angles.

2.—That increase in length of the projectile, while adding to its efficiency as a shell, increases also the penetrative power.

3.—That the amount of rotation adopted is sufficient to ensure the long projectiles striking "end on," and, consequently, to accumulate the whole energy of the mass on the reduced area of the flat front.

In the year 1862 I made experiments with a hardened steel bullet fired from my rifle, and penetrated an iron plate ½-inch thick at an angle of 45°. The bullet had a flat head, and passed through the plate, whereas an ordinary bullet with a rounded point glanced off just as in the present instance.

The results obtained with the 3-pounder gun coincide very closely with those obtained from a rifle, and, as already stated, I have found that whatever I could do with guns of small calibre on my system could be reproduced in the larger sizes on a proportionate scale. This is one advantage inherent to a uniform system of construction and rifling.

The form of the head is the main point to be regarded, and the trial shows that a projectile of fluid-compressed steel, with an ogival-pointed head is deflected in the same manner as the service projectile.

I affirm that the total amount of damage produced by a flat-headed projectile, in causing what the Americans call a *smashing effect* upon a plate, is much greater than that produced by a pointed one. In actual warfare a projectile would rarely impinge on an armour plate perpendicularly to its surface. I have been frequently told by sailors that "*oblique*" fire at sea will be the rule, and "direct" fire the exception; and yet a system is adopted which is useless for any but direct fire. The persistence with which oblique firing has been avoided by all Ordnance Committees impresses one with the idea, which I trust is unfounded, that they are fully aware of a difficulty which they dislike facing.

Penetration by Large Guns.

The 9-inch guns, made on the Whitworth system, weigh 15 tons each, and are capable of firing powder charges of 50 lbs. A 9-inch armour shell, 5 diameters long, weighs 535 lbs., and will contain a bursting charge of 25 lbs.

I have no hesitation in saying that such projectiles would pierce the side of a ship, even though plated with heavy armour, *at some depth below the water-line*, at a distance of 2,000 yards. The 11-inch guns will weigh 27 tons, and will be capable of firing 90 lbs. powder charges. The 11-inch shells, 5 diameters long, will weigh 965 lbs. and contain bursting charges of 45 lbs. They would pierce the side of the ship Hercules, plated with 9-inch armour, at a distance of 2,000 yards.

Four guns of 12-inch bore have been put on board the Monarch. They weigh 25 tons each, and charges of 50 lbs. and 67 lbs. have been fired from them with projectiles of 600 lbs. weight. I have no doubt that these guns have been made with all possible care, and are as strong as their material and construction admits; but if the weight of these guns were in proportion to the capacity of their bore, and if the material were the best that our metallurgical skill could supply for such a purpose, they ought to consume charges of 117 lbs. of powder, and to fire projectiles of 1,250 lbs. weight. They would then be efficient weapons; but at present they are more formidable in name than in reality.

In March 1870 a 9-inch armour-shell, 3½ diameters long, and made of fluid-compressed steel, was fired at a distance of 200 yards, against the War Office shield.

The shell weighed 404 lbs., its length was 31½ inches, and the powder charge was 50 lbs.

The shield was composed of three 5-inch iron plates interlaminated with two 5-inch layers of iron concrete, the whole forming a mass 25 inches thick.

The penetration was 25½ inches; a portion of the rear end of the shell, measuring 6 inches, was left protruding, but perfect, and was neither broken nor upset, but remained a most striking illustration, *which has never been equalled*, of the power of the 9-inch Whitworth gun.

The Length and Rotation of Projectiles.

In 1856 I demonstrated, in the gallery at Manchester, that a rifle bullet, to give the best possible results, should be 3 diameters long. All subsequent experiments with guns have confirmed the soundness of this conclusion. The rule holds good for a 35-ton gun as well as for a rifle.

The drawing represents a series of projectiles, beginning with a rifled sphere and passing on through lengths of 2, 3, 3½, 4, 5, 6, and 7 diameters.

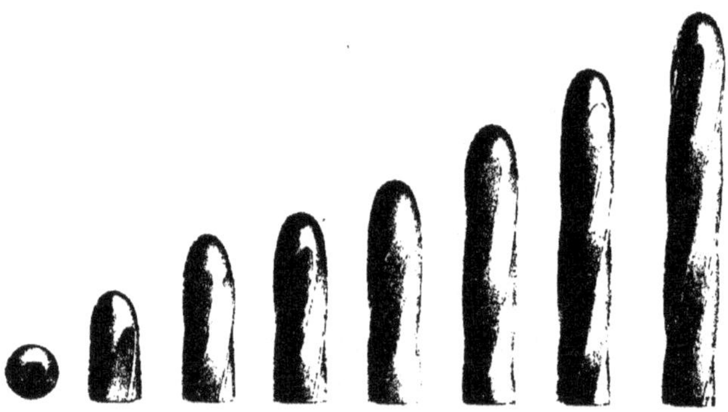

A longer projectile is heavier, its initial velocity is diminished, but its momentum and power of penetration are increased. It remains a longer time in the gun, the powder is more perfectly consumed, a larger charge can be burnt, and the work done in projecting the shot is greater.

It is true that the increased weight of the shot causes a greater strain upon the gun, thereby rendering it dangerous to fire long projectiles from weak uncertain guns.

With a sound material, such as fluid-compressed steel, it becomes possible, by providing for the extra recoil, and giving sufficient rotation, to fire projectiles of any desired length. It has already been stated that long projectiles cannot be fired unless they have a high rotation. The hexagonal system gives the necessary rotation in the most simple manner, but the studded system, with its slow rotation, does not permit the use of these long and powerful projectiles.

For the penetration of armour plates, and where large bursting charges are of importance, I should fire projectiles at least 3½ diameters long, with charges 50 per cent. greater than those now used in the service guns.

It is a common error to estimate the power of a gun by taking the velocity of the shot a distance of a few yards from the gun. In the year 1862 I sent to Shoeburyness a series of projectiles, viz., a sphere, and others 1½, 2, 2½, and 3 diameters long; the respective velocities near the muzzle of the gun were 2,210 feet, 1,905 feet, 1,653 feet, 1,464 feet, and 1,350 feet, whereas the most effective projectile for a moderate range was that of 3 diameters in length.

The firing of rifled spheres is a matter of considerable importance. I have frequently loaded a gun with 6 rifled spheres, which fly together like a covey of partridges, and would prove very formidable in attacking an enemy's boats. The practice required for gunners may also be made with rifled spheres, by loading the gun with only one-third of the usual charge of powder, and a considerable saving of ammunition may thereby be effected.

In the year 1866 some experiments were made at Southport with the view of determining for artillery the points of construction which had been previously established for a rifle. It will be understood that the mechanical conditions for a projectile of iron are different from those for a projectile of lead.

The experiments relating to the best twist of rifling were made with four 1-pounder guns, rifled to pitches of 1 turn in 10, 20, 30, 45 inches, the last named being the proportionate pitch of the service guns. The bore was hexagonal, the maximum and minimum diameters being 1.1945 inches and 1.32 inches.

The projectiles varied in length from 1 to 7 diameters.

With 1 turn in 10 inches all the projectiles went steadily with the point first.

With 1 turn in 20 inches the projectile became unsteady when more than 6 diameters in length.

With 1 turn in 30 inches it fell over when more than 5 diameters in length.

With 1 turn in 45 inches the projectiles turned over, and flew very wild, when more than 3 diameters in length.

The conclusion was, that unless a gun was rifled with a quick pitch, so as to give a high rotation to the projectile, it would not be possible to fire long projectiles.

The rate of rotation which I employ amounts, in the case of some projectiles, to 6,000 revolutions per minute. In machinery 2,000 revolutions per minute would be an extremely high velocity. If regard be had to the energy stored up in a heavy mass of steel, having an onward motion at the rate of 60,000 feet per minute, and performing 6,000 rotations in the same time, some idea may perhaps be formed of the power of the projectile, and the mind may be prepared to understand how the resistance of thick armour plates is overcome when such enormous velocities are suddenly brought to a standstill.

The ranges obtained in the above-mentioned experiments are shown by the annexed table :—

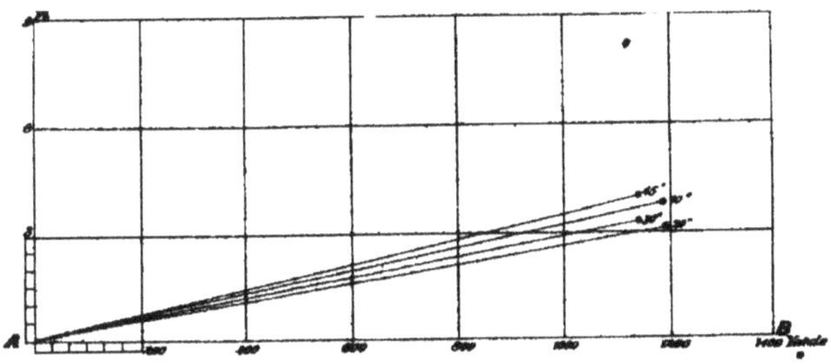

The horizontal line A B, is on a scale of 400 yards to 1 inch, whereas the vertical line, employed to tabulate the deviations, is on a scale of 2 yards to 1 inch. The powder charge was 2½ ounces, and the angle of elevation was 3°. The numbers distinguish the pitches of rifling, and the deflections and ranges were :—

Pitch of Rifling.	Range in Yards.	Deflection.
1 in 10	1,195	1.26 yds.
1 „ 20	1,196	1.03 „
1 „ 30	1,128	1.06 „
1 „ 45	1,147	1.32 „

Projectile 10 Diameters in Length.

In the year 1856, by the desire of Lord Hardinge, a service brass howitzer was rifled on the Whitworth system, and a projectile, 10 diameters in length and weighing 150 lbs., was fired from it at high angles of elevation.

At an elevation of 15°, and with a charge of 9 ounces of powder, the projectile was sent a distance of 470 yards. On a subsequent occasion I showed this shell to Lord Palmerston, at my works in Manchester; he was much impressed, and recognised the importance of firing long projectiles.

The maximum diameter of the shot was 4.48 inches, the minimum diameter being 3.98 inches. The pitch of rifling was 1 turn in 40 inches, and the trial was intended to demonstrate that there was no difficulty in firing shells of any required length.

In 1860 Sir Harry Smith and other officers saw a shell of this length fired at high elevations in my grounds, near Manchester.

Relation of Weight of Projectile to Powder Charge.

Another series of experiments related to the best weight of projectile for a given powder charge.

The gun was a 1-pounder, 50 inches long in the bore, the pitch of rifling being 1 turn in 20 inches, the charge of powder 2½ ounces, and the angle of elevation 3°.

The projectiles weighed 7½, 10, 15, 20, 25, 30, 35, and 40 ounces respectively, and the results of the trials are presented to the eye by a diagram which is on the same scale as before.

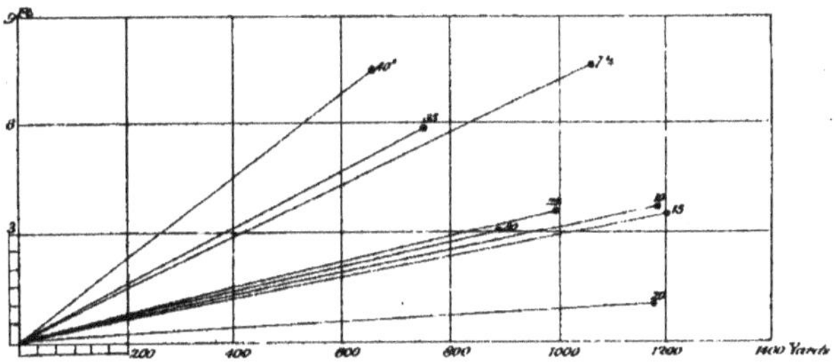

The best result for range and accuracy combined was obtained with the 20 oz. projectile.

The table gives the range and deflection of each projectile.

Weight of Projectiles.	Range in Yards.	Deflection.
7½ oz.	1,048	2.55 yds.
10 ,,	1,183	1.21 ,,
15 ,,	1,205	1.17 ,,
20 ,,	1,153	0.34 ,,
25 ,,	990	1.19 ,,
30 ,,	911	1.07 ,,
35 ,,	742	1.9 ,,
40 ,,	655	2.4 ,,

Influence of the Length of the Gun.

These experiments were made with a 1-pounder gun formed in four lengths, so that by unscrewing the couplings which connected the several parts, the length of the gun could be reduced from 50 inches to 40, 30, and 20 inches at pleasure.

The gun is shown in the annexed illustration :—

The pitch of the rifling was 1 turn in 20 inches, the projectiles were all 3 diameters in length, the powder charge was 2½ ounces, and the angle of elevation 3°.

The subjoined table gives the mean result of 5 rounds fired from each length of gun :—

Length of Gun.	Range in Yards.	Deflection.
50	1,165	1.09 yds.
40	1,184	1.25 ,,
30	1,137	1.64 ,,
20	875	1.95 ,,

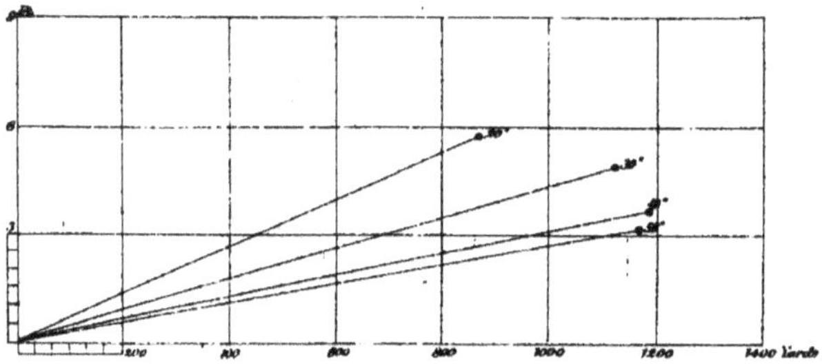

The ranges with lengths of gun equal to 50, 40, and 30, were not very unequal, but there was a great fall with the short gun of 20 inches.

Centreing of the Shot in the Bore.

In the polygonal system the projectile centres itself, that is, it rises so that its axis coincides with the axis of the gun, and it is propelled through the bore with a steady equable motion.

The power of centreing depends on the difference between the maximum and minimum diameters, and also on the direction of the surface which lies between them.

In the hexagonal system there is *sufficient difference* between the maximum and minimum diameters to give all that is required; and the windage being small in proportion, in consequence of the accuracy attainable by this simple geometrical form, the shot cannot pass through the bore without being lifted so as to centre itself.

In the stud system the difference between the maximum and the minimum diameters is *very small*, the length of the stud is so short that the barrel has *little hold* of the projectile, the centreing therefore remains uncertain, and an irregular or wabbling motion is set up while the shot is being propelled through the bore.

Finally, whatever be the windage, an hexagonal shot must centre itself, and the effect of too much windage is *merely a loss* of propelling force; whereas, in the stud system there is both a loss of force and an increased irregularity in motion, due to the defective centreing.

For a 9-inch projectile on the hexagonal system the windage has been .035 of an inch, that for the same projectile in the service being .08 of an inch.

I almost entirely avoid the loss of power by windage in my breech-loading gun; of which a description is given in Chapter III.

EXPERIMENT WITH 2½-POUNDER WHITWORTH MOUNTAIN GUN, 1.9 INCHES BORE, FIRED WITH THE AXIS HORIZONTAL TO SHOW THE DIFFERENCE IN RANGE BETWEEN THE GUN RECOILING IN A FIXED TUBE IN THE DIRECTION OF ITS AXIS, AND THE SAME GUN FIRED FROM AN ORDINARY FIELD CARRIAGE OF TEAK-WOOD, AND FROM A FIELD CARRIAGE OF WHITWORTH METAL.

POWDER CHARGE, 8 OZ. PROJECTILE, TAPER REAR, WEIGHT, 2½ LBS.

POINT STRUCK AT EACH RANGE 10 INCHES BELOW AXIS.

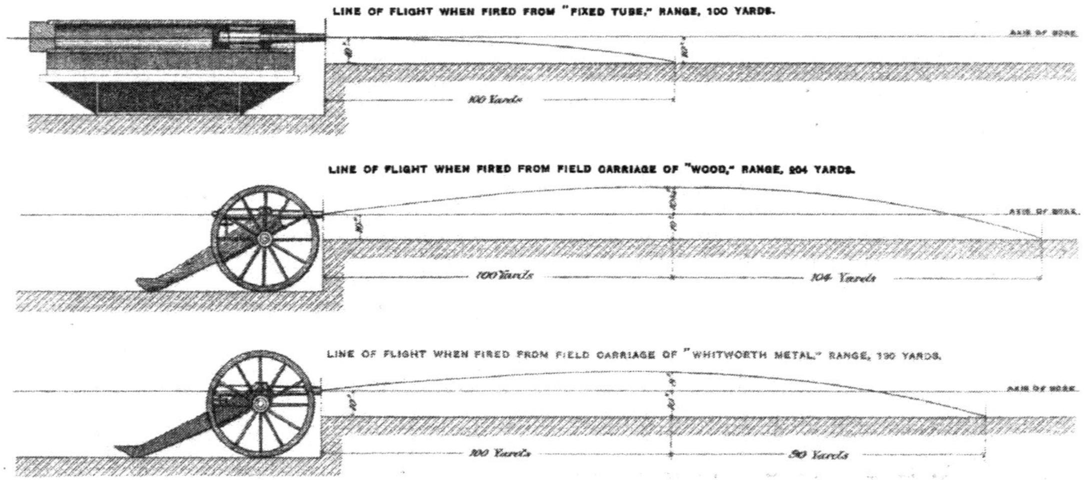

SCALE FOR RANGE, 1 INCH = 45 YARDS.
SCALE FOR HEIGHT, 1 INCH = 5 FEET.

Influence of Rigidity in the Carriage.

The annexed diagram gives the result of some remarkable experiments made on the influence of rigidity in the carriage of a gun.

1.—A 2½-pounder Whitworth mountain gun was first placed in a tube, with its axis coincident with that of the tube. On firing, the gun could only recoil in the exact line of the axis of the tube. The shot left the tube in a horizontal line, and its range was 100 yards.

2.—The same gun was then mounted on a field carriage of wood, and laid in a horizontal line. The elasticity of the carriage now came into play; the axis of the gun deflected upwards on recoiling, and the range was 204 yards. The projectile rose to a height of 10¾ inches above the horizontal line of fire.

3.—The gun was finally mounted on a field carriage of Whitworth metal. Here its axis is brought much nearer to the axle of the carriage, and the leverage which assists the deflection is correspondingly reduced; also the rigid steel yields less than the wood.

The gun was laid, as before, in a horizontal line, and its axis deflected upwards, but to a less extent. The range was 190 yards, but the shot rose above the line of fire to a height of only 8 inches instead of 10¾ inches. The trajectory with a nearly equal range was therefore much flatter, and the experiment is most instructive as demonstrating the influence of the carriage upon the trajectory of a gun.

COMPARISON OF HEXAGONAL AND STUDDED PROJECTILES.

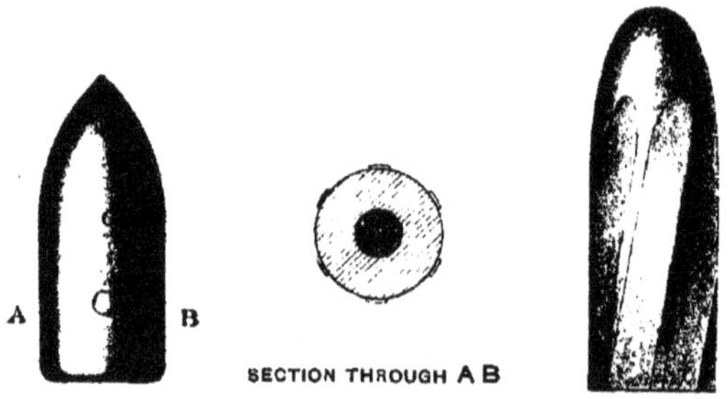

9-INCH "STUDDED" PROJECTILE. 9-INCH "HEXAGONAL" PROJECTILE

SCALE $\frac{1}{16}$.

The annexed sketch shows an hexagonal rifled projectile for a 9-inch gun, and a service Palliser studded projectile for grooved gun of the same bore. The studs are 12 in number and are indicated in the drawing.

In order to contrast the two systems, viz., the French studded system adopted at Woolwich, and the polygonal system, I may state that the 12 studs of a 9-inch Palliser projectile have a circumferential area of 18 inches for supporting the shot, but the area of the sides of the six rear studs, by which alone the rotary motion is given, is only 1.6 inches.

No practical engineer would, if he could avoid it, provide so small a surface as 1.6 inches to give even a moderate amount of rotation to a body weighing 250 lbs., much less when the rotation of the shot at the muzzle of the gun has to be at the rate of about 2,500 revolutions per minute. In my 9-inch hexagonal projectiles the rifled surfaces, which both support and rotate the shot, have an area of 187 inches. The increasing pitch which has been adopted for some guns prevents the use of more than one stud in each groove for giving rotation. This ever-varying curve embodies the worst possible method of imparting rotation, for the variation of the curve prevents each rear stud from bearing against the side of the groove of the gun in more than a line of its surface. The excessive pressure may, no doubt, increase the bearing surface, but it can only do so by distorting the soft metal; the shot is then liable to injury, and some accident may ensue. The greater the amount of windage, the greater will be the liability to accident.

The studded system originated with the French, who were compelled, in the first instance, to adopt it, because the studs could be put in separately by hand labour. At that time there was no special machinery for producing a curved surface on the shot itself. This consideration furnishes the only excuse for the use of studded projectiles.

If the grooves were uniform in twist, and a sufficient number of studs were inserted, the system would work, but the expense would be enormous.

Finally, I would state that I know of nothing in mechanics so absurd as the employment of a single row of studs for producing rotation in a shot weighing 150 lbs. The bearing surface on each stud is little more than a line, and the curve upon which the studs act is a varying curve. Mechanicians are well aware of the importance of adequate bearing surface, and, in the construction of machinery, there has of late years been a continual increase in the amount of bearing surface.

Economy of Production.

Another consideration, of the highest importance in relation to the construction of artillery, is economy of production. Hexagonal projectiles for field guns are moulded by my self-acting machinery, which gives an uniform density of sand in the mould, and ensures such perfect regularity in the size of the projectiles, that they can be fired *as they are cast*, just as in the case of spherical shot in smooth bores.

In shaping a large projectile of, say 150 lbs. weight, suitable for a 7-inch gun, the two surfaces are formed, one by a broad-cutting tool ground to a straight line, the other by a hollow tool which rounds the circular portion. These surfaces are produced in a machine at the same time, the shot being rotated according to the pitch as it traverses. The result is that the projectile may be shaped from the casting and made of the exact size to fit the bore of the gun, by an operation lasting 12 minutes, the wages cost of which is 2½d.

Not only is there a considerable saving in the first cost of manufacture with my projectiles, but they require less care and expense in transport, and can be used over and over again for practice. The ordinary studded shot and shell are far more costly, on account of the additional expense of preparing, fitting, and planing the studs. They also require great care in transport, and cannot be used after firing without being re-studded. A saving in the expense of ammunition is material, for it will be found that the cost of the projectiles fired from a gun during its existence is commonly much greater than that of the gun itself.

As compared with the system at present adopted for the service, everything in my system is cheaper, except the gun and the armour-plate shell, both of which are made of steel, a superior, and as regards first cost, a comparatively expensive material, but against such first expense must be set off the fact that it possesses twice the strength of iron, and admits the employment of powder charges with elongated projectiles, such as no one would dare to fire from the service guns.

On the Proof of Guns.

I consider that the present system of proving guns is erroneous, because it is quite possible, according to the service system, to produce permanent injury to a gun without any one being aware of the harm which has been done.

The proof by measurement is the only method which gives the actual strength of a gun without injuring it, and one mode of applying this principle of measurement is the following :—

1.—With a Whitworth measuring instrument, ascertain the exact size of the bore at a given distance from the end, say about the junction of the powder charge and the shot.

2.—Load the gun with the ordinary weight of shot, and with one-half the quantity of powder which it is known that the gun can properly consume. I call the full quantity of powder the *proper charge*.

3.—Measure the bore, after firing, in the same place, as before.

4.—If no disturbance of the metal has taken place increase the charge of powder, and continue to fire increased charges until the proper charge has been fired. The gun is measured after each discharge, and there ought to be no undue or permanent enlargement.

5.—Then fire an increasing weight of shot with the proper charge of powder, until a sensible enlargement, not due to wear, has been produced.

The limit of endurance has now been reached, and the greatest charge that can be employed without permanent injury to the gun has been ascertained.

6.—Unless it be desired to test the ultimate strength of the gun, the firing of two shot of the ordinary weight, with the proper charge of powder, will be a sufficient test that the gun is capable of sustaining its regulation or proper charge of powder and shot.

Another mode of proof, upon the same principle, which I have lately adopted for my guns, consists in preventing the shot from moving when the powder is ignited, the gases generated by the explosion escaping only through the vent.

I have found that about one-sixth of the regular powder charge fired in this way gives the same strain to the gun as a full charge fired in the ordinary manner. To prevent the movement of the shot, a screw is cut on the periphery of the gun, at the muzzle, and on it is fitted a screwed cap, having a solid end. The gun is loaded with a cartridge of the ordinary length, but containing one-sixth of the regular charge, and supported by tin discs in the centre of the bore; a flat-fronted shot with tight wads to prevent any escape of gas, and a round steel bar, reaching from the shot to the end of the bore, are introduced, and the cap with the solid end is screwed on.

The gun is then ready for firing, after which my measuring instrument is introduced into the bore, and any enlargement, to the ten-thousandth of an inch in extent, may be ascertained.

If there be no enlargement, the powder charges may be gradually increased until a slight enlargement has been produced. The real strength of the gun is thus positively ascertained, and should be recorded and stamped upon each gun. This would give confidence to the gunners, and would act as a check upon those engaged in the manufacture.

When the ultimate endurance of any particular kind of gun is thus to be ascertained, the regular powder charges, or any quantity deemed desirable, may be used, the enlargements being recorded after each discharge.

By this method of proving the endurance, the enormous cost at present incurred may be saved, and I would observe that the present mode of proving guns for endurance, with a less weight of powder and shot than that which is known to be most effective, tends to mislead, and is a waste of ammunition. In the "*Times,*" March 16th, 1869, an account is given of the "Endurance of the 9-inch Woolwich Gun," according to which 19 *tons of powder were consumed in the trial,* but as more than half the rounds fired were with powder charges only about one-half the most effective charge, and the remainder with three-quarters the charge, while *all* the shot fired were only two-thirds the best weight for that size of bore, I contend that the trial afforded no proper test of endurance, but was a sheer waste of ammunition. What would be thought of testing a cable with half the strain it ought to bear one hundred times?

CHAPTER III.

It having now been proved that guns made of fluid-compressed steel are capable of firing longer projectiles, and of resisting much greater charges of powder than can be consumed in a gun loaded at the muzzle, I pass on to describe the mechanical features of the 9-pounder breech-loading gun and carriage, which was exhibited, during the year 1872, at South Kensington, and of which a public trial was made at Southport on October the 8th and 9th, 1872.

The following challenge was placed upon the gun:—This gun will be fired on the sands at Southport, Lancashire, the latter end of September. Messrs. Joseph Whitworth and Co. will be glad to compete with any British or foreign gun and carriage of the same weight, for range, accuracy, penetration, and rapidity of firing.

This gun is made of fluid-compressed steel, and the breech is closed by a heavy sliding block of the same material, working between two portions of the breech end of the gun, under and over the sliding block, which may be called block guides. The faces of the block guides are grooved with a number of parallel grooves, the upper and lower surfaces of the block being similarly formed, and inclined at a very small angle to a plane perpendicular to the axis of the gun, thus forming a portion of a screw thread, which would be traced upon a cylinder of extremely large radius. These threads constitute what may be called a "straight-line screw," having their sides nearest the muzzle undercut, so that when the heavy strain, resulting from firing the charge comes upon the block, there may be no tendency to force the block guides apart; but, on the contrary, they are more tightly held.

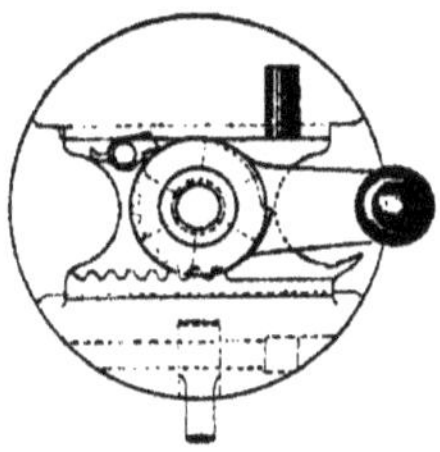

END VIEW, BREECH CLOSED.

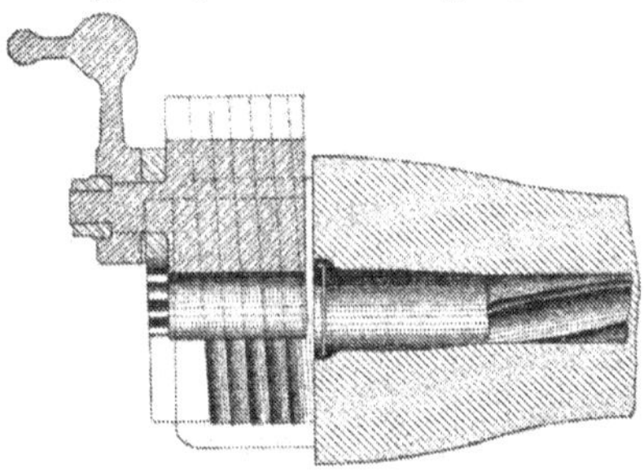

LONGITUDINAL SECTION, BREECH OPEN.

The powder chamber is enlarged in diameter and reduced in length, being 2¼ diameters long, and containing a charge of 50 per cent. more powder than the service charge of a muzzle loader. There is also a slightly enlarged shot chamber to ensure ease in loading. The enlargement of the shot chamber permits of the reduction of the windage in a degree which could not otherwise be attained. In this gun the enlargement is .03 of an inch, the remaining part of the bore having windage of .01 of an inch.

The sliding breech block is shaped at the side, so as to form a part of a tube of the same diameter as the powder chamber; the hollowed out side of the block forms a prolongation of the powder chamber when the breech is open.

For the convenience of loading it is desirable to fit an inner guide into the tubular part, corresponding with the bore of the piece, and similarly rifled, and through this rifled guide piece the projectile is passed into the shot chamber. The guide piece is not, however, absolutely necessary, as the gun can be loaded without it, and in all cases it is removed before the powder cartridge is inserted. The breech block is movable horizontally, and the small obliquity of the threads causes it to tighten itself with sufficient force against the rear end of the gun. It is readily moved to and fro, and provides a large amount of bearing surface for resisting the explosion; the bearing surface in this gun being 30.24 inches, which is three times greater than that which supports the vent piece in the service breech loader of the same calibre. The breech block is worked by means of a rack and pinion, a stud being formed on the back of the breech block, and a weighted hand lever being mounted upon it; on the same stud a pinion is mounted, which gears with a rack fixed upon the lower guide of the breech block. The pinion is worked by the hand lever, the handle and pinion have interlocking projections, allowing, however, the handle some freedom of motion, so that it may be used with a hammer-like action to start the breech block.

The mechanical features of the breech loader may be recapitulated briefly as follows:—

1.—A heavy breech piece with a large area of bearing surface.

2.—An enlarged diameter of powder chamber.

3.—A slightly enlarged shot chamber.

4.—A diminished windage in the bore of the gun.

The carriage like the gun is also made of "fluid-compressed steel," and has the trail formed by side plates, connected at the rear ends by a metal shoe, and at intervals by cross pieces or stays. The bearings in which the trunnion arms rest, are forged solid with the side plates. The axle passes through the side plates immediately beneath the trunnion of the gun, and through a flanged tube, which is fitted and bolted between the side plates, and forms the main stay. The ends of the axle are coned to receive the wheels, which are bushed with brass, and on each end of the axle a screw thread is cut; a nut on this thread, when screwed up, binds the wheel tightly between two collars upon the axle, and resists by friction the tendency of the wheels to revolve when the gun recoils on firing. The screws on the axle are right and left handed, whereby the recoil tends to tighten the nuts.

In order to elevate the gun, a forked lever is jointed to the side plates, just below the axle, and this lever, at its rear end, carries a trunnion nut, in which a hand screw works. The screw is carried by a collar provided with studs or trunnions on either side, which are received into a cross piece connecting the two side plates, and secured there by a cap. The forked lever is connected with the breech end of the gun by a rod, which is pin jointed, both to the lever and to the gun. The connecting rod has two or more pin holes in it, and by shifting the pin connecting the rod with the lever from one hole to another, an increased range of elevation is obtained. On either side of the gun, metal ammunition boxes are hung, the axle passing through the middle of the box.

By this construction of carriage the gun is brought down very close to the axle, and consequently less strain is thrown upon the frame, the recoil taking place nearly in a straight line.

Whitworth 9-Pounder Breech-Loading Field Gun.

Gun :—

		Cwts.	Qrs.	Lbs.
Length over all	79.75″			
,, of Bore	66.275″			
Diameter of Bore major	2.74″			
Pitch of Rifling—1 turn in 18.2 calibres.				
Weight of gun complete		8	3	0

Carriage :—

		Cwts.	Qrs.	Lbs.
Diameter of wheels	58″			
Extreme elevation of gun	34°			
Weight of trail on ground		1	0	0
,, Limber hook		0	3	0
,, Carriage complete		10	0	0

TRIALS OF 9-POUNDER AT SOUTHPORT IN 1872.

The following details show the nature of some of the trials made at Southport, with the 9-pounder breech-loading field gun, on the 8th and 9th of October, 1872.

Invitations to witness these trials were issued to engineers, military officers, and other gentlemen.

For testing range and accuracy, six rounds of solid shot, 4 diameters in length and tapered at the rear, were fired at an elevation of 40°, each shot weighing 12 lbs. 9 oz., powder charge 2¼ lbs. R. L. G. The form of shot is seen from the illustration :—

Round.	Elevation.	Range in yards.	Deflection in feet.	Direction of Wind.
1	40°	10,320	41 right.	
2	"	10,100	40 "	
3	"	10,305	46 "	
4	"	10,304	47 "	
5	"	10,111	44 "	
6	"	10,220	50 "	
Mean range and deflection		10,226	44.6 "	
Mean variation in range and deflection		98	3	

The above ranges were considerably affected, both in accuracy and length, by the gusty wind blowing in an unfavourable direction.

The following results had been obtained on a previous trial with three rounds fired at the same elevation, the projectiles and powder charges being unchanged :—

Round.	Elevation.	Range in yards.	Deflection in feet.	Direction of Wind.
1	40°	10,500	531 right.	
2	„	10,600	528 „	
3	„	10,515	510 „	
Mean range and deflection		10,538	523 „	
Mean variation in range and deflection		41	9	

Ten rounds of common shells, $3\frac{1}{2}$ diameters in length, and tapered at the rear end, were then fired at an elevation of 10°, each shell weighing 9 lbs., powder charge $2\frac{1}{4}$ lbs. R. L. G. The form of shell is seen by the illustration :—

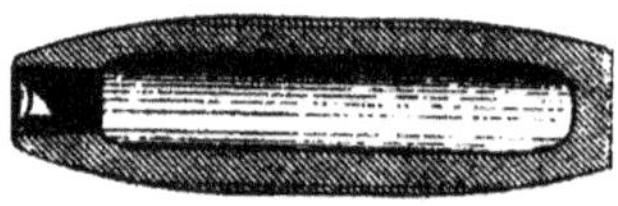

Round.	Elevation.	Range in yards.	Deflection in feet.	Direction of Wind.
1	10°	4,314	4 left.	
2	„	4,468	12 „	
3	„	4,357	3 „	
4	„	4,339	9 „	
5	„	4,300	18 „	
6	„	4,468	6 „	
7	„	4,431	14 „	
8	„	4,251	13 „	
9	„	4,350	14 „	
10	„	4,310	8 „	
Mean range and deflection		4,359	10 left.	
Mean variation in range and deflection		53.8	4.1	

Then five rounds of common shells, $3\frac{1}{2}$ diameters in length, with parallel rears, were fired at an elevation of 3 degrees, each shell weighing 9 lbs., powder charge $2\frac{1}{4}$ lbs. R. L. G. The illustration shows the shell in section.

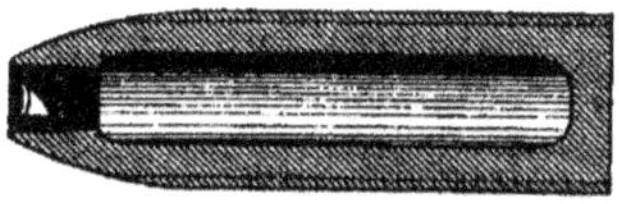

Round.	Elevation.	Range in yards.	Deflection in feet.	Direction of Wind.
1	3°	1,928	On line.	
2	„	1,911	1 left.	
3	„	2,030	3 „	
4	„	1,860	1 right.	
5	„	1,925	8 „	
Mean range and deflection		1,931	1 right.	
Mean variation in range and deflection		40	2.8	

In order to test for penetration, a flat-fronted steel shell, 5 diameters in length, was fired at an armour plate 3 inches in thickness (purchased from Messrs. Cammels), placed at a distance of 300 feet from the gun, and inclined at 45° to the line of fire; the shell weighing 16 lbs. 1 oz.; powder charge $2\frac{3}{4}$ lbs. R. L. G.

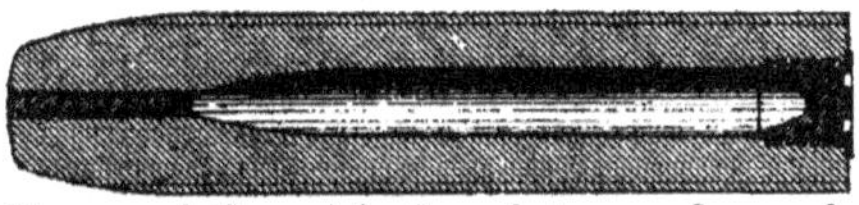

The shell passed through the plate, as shown in the diagram, and went into the sand butt behind to a distance of 5 feet.

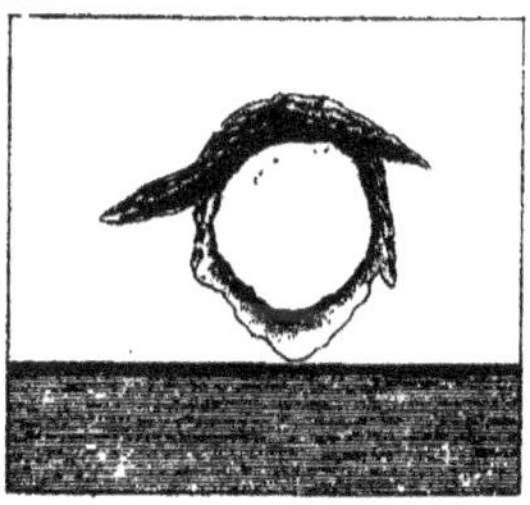

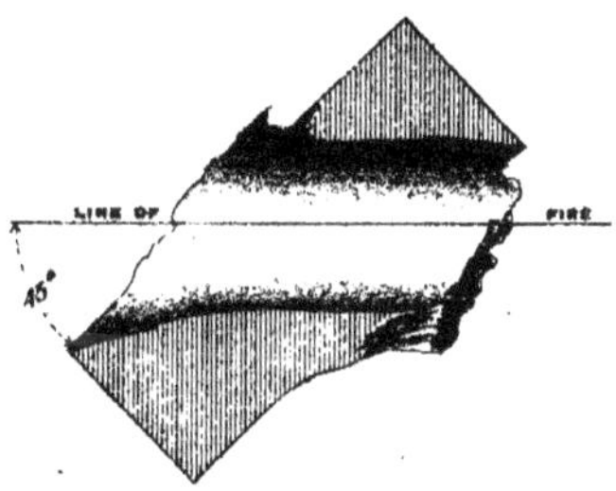

Comparison of Trajectories.

The excellence of a rifled gun is very properly estimated by the flatness of the trajectory, or path described by the shot, at small elevations.

If there were no atmosphere, the trajectory at any given range, say of 500 yards, could be easily calculated when the velocity of projection was ascertained. The bullet would rise above a horizontal plane through the point of projection to a height equal to that through which it would fall from rest under the action of gravity in half the time of flight. It is evident that the time of flight would be less with a greater velocity of projection, and that the flatness of the trajectory depends on the rapidity of the flight over a given range. In the theoretical case referred to, conceive that the velocity of projection is 1,000 feet per second, and the range 500 yards, the bullet would rise to a height of 9 feet before its path began to curve downwards.

The resistance of the atmosphere entirely upsets the simplicity of this calculation. The exact trajectory of a projectile can only be ascertained by direct experiment, but it is clear that the trajectory will be improved if the shot retains its initial velocity of projection with but small diminution. This is one reason why a projectile 3 diameters long gives a flat trajectory, the prejudicial resistance of the air has less effect upon it than it would have on a shorter projectile of the same weight, which exposes a larger sectional area to the action of the atmosphere.

By experiments made at the rifle gallery, I have ascertained that the trajectory of a bullet fired from the Whitworth rifle, and ranging 500 yards, is given by a line rising 7 feet 6 ins. above the horizontal plane, whereas that obtained from the Enfield rifle, at the same range, with the same powder charge, and with a bullet of like weight, is given by a line rising 11ft. 10in. above the horizontal plane.

The low trajectory given by the Whitworth rifle is a most important element in considering its practical value. The great difficulty experienced in the use of the rifle for long distances consists in the utter inability of any marksman to judge correctly the distances of objects far away; this difficulty can only be met by causing the projectile to move in a trajectory or path as low and level as possible, whereby it becomes possible to hit objects of moderate height within the range of the weapon.

The data for ascertaining the precise form of the trajectory in the case of the Whitworth 9-pounder gun are not determined, but a comparison may be instituted between the Whitworth new 9-pounder breech-loading guns and Woolwich 9-pounder muzzle-loading guns, which proves the great superiority of the former weapon.

It will be seen from the annexed table that the range of the Whitworth 9-pounder at 1° of elevation is very nearly the same as that of the Woolwich 9-pounder at an elevation of 2°. The range of the Whitworth gun at 4° is greater than that of the Woolwich gun at 6°, and so for other elevations. The gun which ranges 1,000 yards at an elevation of 1° must have a flatter trajectory than another which is fired at a double elevation in order to obtain the same range. The performance of the Whitworth gun is derived from experiments made on the 27th of August, 1872; that of the Woolwich gun is taken from experiments made at Shoeburyness on the 23rd of April, 1869, and published in "*The Standard,*" for the 26th of April, 1869.

Comparative ranges obtained with the 9-pounder Whitworth breech-loading gun, and the service muzzle-loading gun of the same calibre :—

Angle of Elevation.	Whitworth breech-loading gun. Powder charge 2¼ lbs. Projectile 9 lbs.	Service muzzle-loading gun. Powder charge 1 lb. 5 ozs. Projectile 9 lbs.
0°	381 yards.	277 yards.
1°	1,018 "	673 "
2°	1,543 "	1,065 "
3°	1,955 "	1,377 "
4°	2,363 "	1,730 "
5°	2,760 "	2,067 "
6°	3,063 "	2,346 "
7°	3,268 "	2,610 "
10°	4,099 "	3,238 "

The dimensions and weight of the Woolwich muzzle-loading service 9-pounder are :—

GUN :—

Length over all ... ... 72.0″
" of bore ... ... 63.5″
Diameter of bore ... 3.0″
Rifling ... ... 3 grooves
Pitch of do., 1 turn in 30 calibres

	Cwt.	Qrs.	Lbs.
Weight of gun	8	0	0

CARRIAGE :—

Diameter of wheels ... 60″
Extreme elevation of gun 21½°

	Cwt.	Qrs.	Lbs.
Weight of trail on ground	1	2	5
Weight of limber hook	1	0	12
Weight of carriage complete ...	10	2	0

The dimensions and weight of the Whitworth breech-loading 9-pounder are :—

GUN :—

Length over all ... 79.75″
" of bore ... 66.275″
Diameter of bore major 2.74″
Pitch of rifling—1 turn in 18.2 calibres.

	Cwt.	Qrs.	Lbs.
Weight of gun complete	8	3	0

CARRIAGE :—

Diameter of wheels ... 58″
Extreme elevation of gun 34°

	Cwt.	Qrs.	Lbs.
Weight of trail on ground	1	0	0
" limber hook	0	3	0
" Carriage complete	10	0	0

Comparison of the Whitworth and Woolwich Guns.

The superiority of steel over iron as a material for the construction of guns, and the advantages of my system, are so indisputable, that in every case a Whitworth steel gun of given calibre is more effective than a Woolwich service gun of larger bore. It is difficult to institute an exact comparison in every case, but I am convinced that the following statement is within the truth, and may be accepted unhesitatingly :—

1.—The Whitworth 3-pounder muzzle-loading gun is better than the service 6-pounder breech-loading gun.

2.—The Whitworth 6-pounder muzzle-loading gun is superior to the Woolwich 9-pounder muzzle-loading gun.

3.—The Whitworth 9-pounder muzzle-loading gun is superior to the service 12-pounder breech-loading gun.

4.—The Whitworth 12-pounder muzzle-loading gun is more effective than a Woolwich 16-pounder muzzle-loading gun.

The experiments about to be detailed, justify, so far as they are complete, the estimate which I have formed.

1.—The Whitworth 3-pounder muzzle-loading gun, fired at Southport in April 1869, gave a range of 1,432 yards at an elevation of 3°. The weight of the gun was 3 cwt. 2 qrs. 7 lbs.

In the treatise on construction and manufacture of the rifled ordnance in the British service, by Captain Stoney, R.A., it is stated on page 229 that a Woolwich bronze 7-pounder gun fired at an elevation of 3° 3′ has a range of only 900 yards.

2.—The Whitworth 6-pounder muzzle-loading gun, fired at Southport in June 1869, gave a range of 1,585 yards at an elevation of 3°. The weight of the gun being 5 cwt. 1 qr. 5 lbs.

The Woolwich 9-pounder muzzle-loading gun, fired at Shoeburyness in April 1869, gave a range of 1,377 yards at an elevation of 3°. The weight of the gun being 8 cwt. 0 qr. 14 lbs.

3.—The Whitworth 9-pounder muzzle-loading gun, fired at Southport in June 1869, gave a range of 1,333 yards at an elevation of 3°, with a projectile 6 diameters in length, weighing 15 lbs.

The same Whitworth gun gave a range of 1,614 yards, at an elevation of 3°, in June 1869. The weight of the gun at this later trial was 8 cwt. 0 qr. 4 lbs., and the weight of the projectile was 9 lbs.

In the treatise by Captain Stoney, R.A., previously referred to, it is also stated on page 222 that a service 12-pounder breech-loading gun, fired at an elevation of 3° 2', has a range of 1,300 yards.

4.—The Whitworth new 12-pounder breech-loading gun, fired at Southport in August 1871, obtained a range of 4,973 yards at an elevation of 10°. The projectile weighed 17⅛ lbs, was 4 diameters in length, and the powder charge was 3½ lbs.

The Woolwich 16-pounder muzzle-loading gun, fired at Shoeburyness in January 1871, gave a range of 3,807 yards at an elevation of 10°. The projectile weighed 16 lbs, and the powder charge was 3 lbs.

Finally, I have to remark, that if a gun be made of a stronger metal, if the system of rifling adopted be in accordance with mechanical laws, and if the gun can consume more powder with less loss of force by windage, it must be a better gun for all purposes, than another which fails to approach it in these essential characteristics.

Accordingly, the best performance in penetration, regard being had to the proportion between the bore of the gun and the thickness of the plate pierced, has been obtained with the Whitworth 12-pounder breech-loading gun of 3 inches bore.

The gun is called a 12-pounder, but I have fired from it a flat-headed steel projectile, 6 diameters in length, and weighing 31 lbs., with a powder charge of $3\frac{3}{4}$ lbs.

The projectile to which I refer, pierced a $4\frac{1}{2}$-inch wrought-iron armour plate, received from J. Brown and Co., of Sheffield, and passed 10 feet 6 inches into the butt supporting the plate. The projectile, with a portion of the plate, was exhibited at South Kensington in 1872. The trial was made in February 1871.

The best performance for range has been obtained by a Whitworth muzzle-loading gun. As stated in page 38, I have obtained at Shoeburyness, with a projectile weighing 250 lbs., the longest range on record, viz., 11,243 yards, or nearly $6\frac{4}{10}$ miles. Here the angle of elevation was 33°, the powder charge being 50 lbs.; but if it had been a breech-loading gun on my principle it would have given a still greater range.

When such results as these are recorded, I would ask if there can remain any doubt as to a system which displays the same uniform and undeviating superiority, whether it be applied to rifled small arms or to the heaviest artillery.

INDEX.

Printed by George Falkner and Son, Imperial Buildings, Deansgate, Manchester.

Lightning Source UK Ltd.
Milton Keynes UK
UKOW06n2156050917
308640UK00001B/60/P

9 781297 71738